SENIOR GUIDE:

DAY-HIKES IN THE
SOUTHWESTERN
NATIONAL PARKS
and
MONUMENTS

James Campbell

WestPark Books
1819 Birdseye Creek Road
Gold Hill, Oregon 97525

ACKNOWLEDGEMENTS

A book like this would never have been possible without the help of many, many people. I especially wish to thank the dozens of National Park Service employees, volunteers, and representives of affiliated Natural History associations who gave me information and insights into their area. They generously took time to consider and correct early drafts of the manuscript, lending their expertise and knowledge. Without exception they represent the highest standards of public service. In an era of low budgets, increased visitation, and decreased staffing, they continue to maintain the lofty ideal that the National Park Service represents.

A second acknowledgement goes to my family, who provided both moral and financial support.

A final, and large, thanks to my editors. Cathy AuBuchon and Susan Morgan took the time and care to correct and clarify the manuscript, magically turning incomplete phrases into real sentences, and finding good homes for dangling participles. This book is for them.

Copyright© 1986 by James Campbell
Cover by Ray Shafer
Printed in USA by Maverick Publications, Bend, OR 97701
Library of Congress Catalog Card Number **85-52137**
International Standard Book Number **0-936205-11-3**

Published by WestPark Books
1819 Birdseye Creek Road
Gold Hill, Oregon 97525

1st Printing-January 1986, 2nd Printing-July 1986

Typography and assistance by Springs Printery and TYPE/LINE, Rogue River, OR 97537.   Manufactured in the United States

CONTENTS

Why Go?
Enjoyment — the Best Part
Recreation and Re-creation
Learning Something New

Some Preliminaries — Getting Ready To Go
Tuning Up
Getting Information
A Word About Maps

First-Aid and Emergency Kit
Getting to the Trailhead — Safe Driving
At the Trailhead — Safe Parking
Equipment Lists for Senior Day-Hikes

Be Prepared for Changing Conditions
The Most Dangerous Condition —
    Hypothermia Weather
Other Weather-Related Hazards
Take It Easy
Questions For You and Your Physician
Trail Techniques to Increase Comfort and Save Energy
A Matter of Attitude

Safety Starts With Good Planning
Weather — Be Ready For A Change
Get Information on Trail Conditions
Plan Your Day-Hikes Around Your Personal Interests
Understand Your Own Limitations
Deciding When To Turn Back
If Your Plans Are Unusual
What To Do If You Become Separated, Lost, Ill,
    or Injured
Avoiding Hazards
Avoiding Things That Bite, Poke, Sting, or
    Otherwise Make You Feel Bad
Injuries Caused By Heat and Cold
Hypothermia
Injuries Caused By Overheating
Other Irritations, Large and Small

PART II

MEET THE SENIOR HIKER

I was hiking out of the Grand Canyon one cold January day when I met The Senior Hiker. I'd camped the night before in the Park Service campground near Phantom Ranch, eight slippery miles and more than a thousand vertical feet from my trailhead on the South Rim. I carried all the usual backpacking equipment, some unnecessary gear and enough winter clothing to keep me warm on an ascent of Mount McKinley. Heavy thick-soled boots protected my feet and ankles from any loose stones marring the smooth trail. I had enough food for at least an extra day or two in the canyon, just on the off-chance I should wander away from the well-traveled path. A two-day water supply sloshed somewhere in the bowels of my pack, insurance against any sudden dry spells.

In spite of the heavy load, I was making reasonable time on a long uphill grade, feeling good and looking good — over-equipped, over-prepared, but mentally alert and at ease with myself and my world. I was a picture of the complete outdoorsman, rugged and ready for anything. Little did I know that I was in for some heavy-duty, industrial-strength re-evaluation.

As I staggered around a switchback, I spotted The Senior Hiker. Instead of a specially-designed, wind-resistant, rain-repellant, nylon-cotton-blend parka overlaying a sixty-dollar natural wool sweater (its loom-mate said to have been to 20,000 feet on Everest), The Senior Hiker was outfitted in a scale-spattered fisherman's jacket, an old sweater, and a synthetic sportshirt. Instead of lug-soled, ankle-high hiking boots of the latest and most expensive design, he was wearing (horrors!) street shoes — low-cut, crepe-soled, dust-over-Shinola street shoes. I was appalled.

More insulting still — instead of an all-new computer-designed backpack boasting a torsoflex suspension-system, conical-shaped waistband and handy removable pockets, he carelessly carried his lunch in a tiny day-pack that rested lightly on his shoulders. The Park Service, I thought, should protect such poor souls from themselves. How could a senior citizen of his obvious years possibly survive a half-day hike into the rugged backcountry of the Grand Canyon? Surely he needed all the essentials a sensi-ble, prudent hiker (like me, for instance) would carry. After all, I most certainly knew what I was doing, but he was just out for a good time. He couldn't be getting any-thing out of his hike — he was having too much fun.

What was supremely aggravating about The Senior Hiker, though, was that he was enjoying himself — at least as much as I, judging from the look of pure pleasure on his face. As I trudged up the trail, I began to contemplate the Lesson of the Senior Hiker — that you don't have to be under fifty and over-equipped to enjoy day-hikes in a national park or monument. I had hiked long distances and camped in the backcountry; he had traveled light and at his own pace. I had chosen one way, he another, and we seemed equally happy with our choices.

My way was to hike for several days, anticipating every need and every possible emergency (even to the point of imagining unlikely and improbable hazards). I went pre-pared for any eventuality, however remote. His approach was somewhat different — he was having a good time, hiking as slowly as he wanted, following his own pace and interests. He was doing something he saw as exciting and enjoyable. I, on the other hand, was making a job out of what should have been fun. Another lesson learned.

The Lesson of The Senior Hiker has stayed with me: take the trail as it comes, take the things required to travel lightly and safely, and enjoy yourself. The Senior Hiker wasn't caught up in the mystique of rugged, consumer-oriented outdoorsmanship.

No, I don't carry my food in a paper sack now, and no, I haven't given up my computer-designed backpack. Frankly, I like it too much and it's too comfortable (and much too expensive) to abandon. I have, though, changed the way I think about Seniors and their enjoyment of day-hikes on the trails of our national parks and monuments.

Thanks to the Senior Hiker, I've expanded my conceptions and ideas about what Seniors are capable of. I've disco-vered that Seniors, regardless of age, can enjoy day-hiking in national parks and monuments, that they don't always have to take overnight hikes to enjoy the solitude of wil-derness. I've learned, too, about national park and monu-ment trails that will absolutely delight Senior hikers. I've discovered that many who haven't tried day-hikes need only a little encouragement and help to hit the trail safely, enjoyably, and comfortably.

I've found an almost universal curiosity about hiking, backcountry use, and wilderness travel among the Seniors I've visited with in national parks and monuments. Some Seniors are just now finding the time and interest to try day-hikes. They've been too busy making a living and raising a family to know firsthand the delight of being on a trail, of learning new things about themselves and their world. Now that they're free to travel, they want to enjoy outdoor experiences on their own.

Safety is a primary consideration, of course, but The Senior Hiker showed me that day-hikes are sometimes more enjoyable if they're approached light-heartedly, without nervous over-preparation. He reminded me that physical hardware sometimes gets in the way of experience, shoving pleasure aside while saddling the Senior with unnecessary responsibilities. He also taught me to simplify my hiking technique so that equipment doesn't interfere with my interests or enjoyment of the trail.

Whoever he was and wherever he is, I hope he has pleasant memories of his day in the Canyon. I'll bet he's still having the time of his life. Senior Hiker, I take off my Gore-Tex holofill-insulated hat to you. You taught me well.

1

DAY-HIKING FOR SENIORS

Seniors are discovering some new and interesting things about themselves and their world. If you're a Senior, you're probably in your fifties, sixties or seventies, active and vigorous, eager to learn and do new things. At last you have leisure to explore our country — really see it first-hand. And you probably want to start with the best and most beautiful — our National Park System.

Seniors love our National Parks and National Monuments, especially those in the Southwest. They find landscapes that uplift the spirit with their openness and beauty, wilderness regions isolated enough to lend perspective to any life, and strands of human history linking us to a nearly forgotten past. Best of all, Seniors are finding that they can get to know southwestern parks and monuments intimately — they're discovering day-hiking.

Seniors enjoy day-hikes. Such hikes aren't expeditions — they don't require the extensive preparation or physical effort of long-distance overnight treks. With a little help, Seniors can tailor their rambles to their own interests, time and physical abilities. They're discovering that day-hikes are not only comfortable, safe and enjoyable, but invigorating to the mind and body as well.

Day-hikes in national parks and monuments are safe and enjoyable, all right, but they do take some effort and planning. They don't have to be drudgery — they should be comfortable and inexpensive enough to enjoy more than once or twice a year. If they aren't, then why attempt them? Day-hikes are safe and agreeable — activities that any Senior with ordinary strength and stamina can handle without cramping either muscles or budgets.

Any Senior can learn to plan a trip, decide on what to take, where to go, what to do, and how to enjoy the trails in a national park or monument. All it takes is a little common sense, some practical information and the desire to get into the out-of-doors. You don't have to be rugged or rich — if those were requirements, most of us would never know the joy of being on the trail.

You don't have to be a born woodsman or confirmed desert-rat either, and you don't have to look or dress like you're posing for a cigarette ad. You already have most of the gear you need, and undoubtedly you have some ideas about which national parks or monuments you'd like to visit. Probably all you need are some hints about how to get started.

WHY GO?

There are plenty of good reasons to explore our national parks and monuments. Some Seniors find self-expression through hiking or backpacking, others like to get close to nature. Some observe wildlife or simply enjoy wandering in forests or deserts. Some climb mountains, others ski down them. No matter what the reason (or excuse), day-hiking in national parks and monuments provide benefits missing from ordinary urban existence — some things we can only find by following the footsteps of The Senior Hiker.

We're products of our age, examples of modern man, severely addicted to travel. We love the sense of movement, of looking over the horizon or around the corner. For our own satisfaction we need to see if pastures really are greener somewhere else.

Why have we developed into peripatetic retirees, civilization's most persistant vagabonds? Maybe it's something in our national makeup, a throwback to our restless ancestors or a response to the semi-myth that we're all descended from a great race of explorers and pioneers. Not true for most of us, of course, but it remains part of our psyche nonetheless.

Most of us spent our lives going to school, earning a living, and raising our families. Now that we've reached our mature years, we're free to travel. At last there's time to visit beautiful and interesting places, time to relax and enjoy them leisurely. We've earned it — now we can slow down and see what we've missed. Maybe that's why we travel, why we hold our national parks and monuments in such esteem.

Whatever the reasons, Seniors enjoy traveling and love visiting national parks. Seniors feel the urge for movement as strongly as anyone else. When that particular itch demands scratching, Seniors take a trip to a National Park or a National Monument. Scratching such an itch seems an innocent pastime. It makes us feel good and causes little if any harm. It makes us more alert, more interested in our world, and best of all — it's fun.

Day-hiking is a delightful way to break the pattern imposed by routine. Since most of us are tied to cities, we're required by habit or circumstance to endure an urban lifestyle. Because of how we're forced to live, we try to pack the greatest contrast into our leisure time. For some of us it means a return to a simpler, more "primitive" way of doing things.

To maintain our perspective, to say nothing of our sanity, we need to know that we have a chance to stand aside from the ordinary, a chance to do things differently for awhile — hiking instead of driving, riding a bike instead of flying, drifting on a rubber raft rather than daydreaming on a crosstown bus, or gliding along on cross-country skis instead of sitting in nervous isolation on a subway. Knowing there's a trail waiting in a national park helps maintain a sound perspective among the hustle and bustle of life in the city.

There's more to it than simple escape, though. Like everyone else, Seniors need the stimulation of new challanges to make their lives truly meaningful. We never know how strong we are if we don't push against something. Day-hiking lets us test our abilities safely and comfortably, at our own pace and following our own interests.

Whether or not we're successful in our daily bread-and-butter existence, we need to make a different test of our humanity from time to time. Human nature, at least the late-twentieth-century variety, seems to need the physical challenge of doing something exuberant and unnecessary, something that isn't absolutely required. For some, day-hiking in a national park offers a chance to kick over the traces and move as freely as we sense we should. And it's certainly cheaper and a lot more fun than hiring a therapist.

ENJOYMENT — THE BEST PART

Enjoyment. That's probably the most important thing. No matter what excuse we use for visiting a national park and taking a day-hike, most of the time it comes down to the fact that we simply want to try it — it sounds like it might be fun.

In fact, part of the enjoyment is just thinking about a day-hike. Deciding which park or monument to visit, what to do, what to take, imagining the trip as it might be — that's exciting in itself. It smacks of expeditions and adventures, of journeys into the unknown, of days when there's freedom and strength enough to do and be just about anything a person imagines.

Most Seniors start with maps. I love maps. They're alive with possibilities. Looking at a map I see places I've never been and anticipate the adventures I'll have getting there. The destination isn't all that important — the trip becomes master of the imagination. Maps, gear, routes, food, the recognition of problems and solutions, the daydreaming that goes into mulling over a map is delightful. It takes me out of the ordinary world into a place where anything reasonable becomes possible and anything possible seems reasonable.

Of course, the day-hike itself may take less time than getting ready for it. And after the hike there's always the recollection of the adventure (trips become adventures — why go if they don't?). Being human, we usually forget hardships, blisters or sore muscles, and recall the beauty of sunsets and the glory of being on the trail. It's part of the package, almost a bonus given for making an effort to understand the outdoors and our place in it.

Every outdoor trip has at least three phases — anticipation, the hike itself, and our recollection of the trip.

Whether it's important to others or not, the way a peak looks when it's washed with alpinglow (or even the sight of a tiny blue flower nodding in the sun) becomes a vital part of our day-hike, captured forever by memory. Maybe it's the mind's way of restoring our perspective, reminding us of what it's like to be really alive. It's certainly part of every outdoor adventure — some would say the most relevant part.

RECREATION AND RE-CREATION

Day-hikes in national parks and monuments offer recreation, certainly, but even more importantly they offer re-creation. The difference is more than just a play on words. We're urbanized, homoginized, pastuerized and cauterized until we've nearly lost touch with our origins, our true home. And man's home for most of his existence has been the wilderness. We need to return there once in awhile, go back and rediscover our roots deep in the soil of wild nature. For our sanity, and the sanity of our society, we must re-create ourselves periodically — a good excuse in itself for getting out of the house and onto a wilderness trail.

We're both part and product of the natural world. Insulated from the realities of nature, it's hard to remember that we're part of a small planet's thin film of living matter, that we must meet the same requirements for life as any other living being. Since we're so removed from the imperatives of nature in our daily lifes, it's necessary for us to remind ourselves that we're nature's children. Few of us have, by necessity, felt the sting of icy rain on our faces, or known the obsessive effect of driving thirst except as part of a game. Society and civilization have cushioned us almost completely from the reality of life, and we may be poorer for it. One doesn't have to endure hardship on a day-hike, of course; it's enlightening, though, to recognize the potential for adversity, and know how to escape it. It makes one humble in the presence of something larger and more powerful.

Since our isolation from nature is so pervasive, it's sometimes hard to see the operation of the natural world, of nature in the raw, beautifully true to its own rules. Day-hikes are an easy way to re-establish contact. By observing nature, we can relearn lessons long forgotten, lessons which carry meaning when we return to our daily routines. We begin to understand what's truly important to living and what are artifacts. We begin to understand the difference between what we need to live and what are simply clumsy additions that we're forever tripping over. I think those are important lessons to relearn.

When Seniors observe themselves in the mirror of the natural world they may see that some things they thought to be essential aren't vital after all. Some are simulations of civilization, some are society's veneer, some are necessary — but we can't know the difference between them until they've been examined. Some people call that process growth, others call it wisdom. Whatever it is, it's an essential part of life.

Sometimes we find, by examining our place in the natural world, that we aren't as central to it's operation as we had thought. Some of us, of an humbler turn-of-mind, discover that we're as important as any other living thing. And a few of us, perhaps the luckiest and wisest, find that we're really part of everything else — truly a remarkable and enlightening discovery.

There's no question that day-hikes let us learn more about ourselves. For instance, we seldom have a chance to test our abilities to the limit. Few of us know how far we can walk, or how much we'll enjoy finding out. After all, it isn't an absolutely essential bit of information — we can function without that knowledge. But most Seniors, I think, are pleasantly surprised to find that their limits are far beyond what they had imagined. There's some strength in knowing that you, in your mature years, can cover five miles and climb five-hundred feet if you want, and that you can get there on your own. Not essential knowledge, that's for sure, but pleasing to know none the less.

LEARNING SOMETHING NEW

Nearly everyone likes to learn something new. Man, after all, is a learning animal. Outdoor travel is a marvelous teacher. New physical and mental skills, like how to pack for a day-hike, or how to tell a chickadee from a sparrow, or how to find your way from one place to another when there aren't any street signs — these are exciting new bits of knowledge to acquire. As a Senior, that knowledge is open to you — at last you have the time and opportunity to learn them.

Some other new skills that come from outdoor travel are more subtle. We soon learn a new set of attitudes, find a new way of looking at things. Seniors rediscover that all life shares the same basic problems and solutions, and that we have to be responsible for ourselves. After all, if you forget to carry a comfortable day-pack with your lunch, water, and an extra sweater, you'll not only be cold and hungry, you'll probably have a sore back in the morning. If you take too much gear, you'll be miserable trying to get all your junk from one place to the next. The idea of taking care of basics first becomes more important on the trail. Food, shelter, warmth, security — these become primary, and the idea that these are the important basics of life carries over into our day-to-day existence.

Another lesson soon learned is that of simplicity. You learn what's necessary and what can be done without. With luck, we learn to be at least a little like The Senior Hiker, satisfied to be going, and satisfied that the going's the significant thing. Like The Senior Hiker, we can learn new things and discover new enjoyment safely and comfortably on the trail.

Grand Canyon National Park   *(NPS photo)*

2

BEFORE YOU GO

Seniors are finding day-hikes in our national parks and monuments safe, enjoyable, and enlightening, no question about that. But if you're like most people interested in the out-of-doors, you'll quickly discover that there are simply too many places to go and things to do. Our continent is blessed with an outstanding diversity of fascinating land-scapes — in spite of the unconscionable efforts of greedy and shortsighted "developers". Many (but unfortunately not all) of these landscapes are represented in our country's "crown jewels" — our National Park System.

North America has some of the most spectacular country in the world, ranging from lordly mountain peaks to beau-tifully subtle prairies, from bare-bones deserts to complex rainforests. No matter where you look, you'll find beauty in the North American landscape; that's truly a remarkable thing in this day and age.

There's a problem, though. Because of the frightening loss of natural landscapes and wilderness ecosystems during this century, you may well be a member of the last genera-tion to see the authentic face of our continent, the last to experience it personally. It's frightening and sad to con-template the wholesale loss of natural areas and wilder-ness — places that retain the beauty of the American scene.

So how do you, a Senior with time enough to look for the best in America, a person still vigorous and willing to learn, decide where to go? First, I think, it's important to understand that there's an almost infinite variety of landscapes available to the Senior outdoor traveler.

If you want mountains, you have them in abundance. If deserts intrigue you, try those; they're probably our most overlooked recreational resource. If you've never hiked along the shores of an ocean or on the fringes of a glacier, these are available, too. Decide what your interests are, then determine how you'll get there and what you'll be able to do as you explore the area you've chosen.

SOME PRELIMINARIES — GETTING READY TO GO

Ah, yes — time. When we're young, hardly anyone has enough of it. Most of us have had to make painful decisions about how far we could go and how much time we could spend in any one area. Remember those rushed vacations you used to take? Those days are over — now you have time enough to see what you've missed.

Even after retirement, though, a Senior hiker will sometimes try to crowd too much into too short a time. He'll drive nineteen hours to get to a national park, then find that he has only ten hours to spend on the trail before driving another nineteen hours back home. And, of course, he soon finds that the trip isn't nearly as enjoyable as he imagined it would be. Take heart — there's a better way to do it.

TUNING UP

First, decide what your interests really are. If you find that you won't have time for a long-distance drive, look around locally for another national park or monument — perhaps one you've heard about for years but haven't visited. If you can't make it to the particular park you've been dreaming about, spend your time preparing for the day when you can finally hike its trails. After all, part of every trip is the delightful anticipation of what's to come. It won't be wasted time, either, since you'll be better prepared to enjoy your dream-trip when it materializes.

Many Seniors find it satisfying to begin day-hiking close to home, getting muscles in tone and learning the basics of walking again. No, hiking the sidewalks of a city park won't be the same as day-hiking a section of Yosemite's John Muir Trail, and a half-hour stroll in a nearby state park might not be the equivilant of an all-day hike among Yellowstone's geysers and hot springs, but it's certainly better than staying home.

Besides, shorter local trips will keep you physically fit and eager for longer, more spectacular trips when you find the time for them. Local trips sharpen your skills, make you a better outdoor traveler, and can be truly enjoyable experiences. And if you make enough of them, you'll soon be known as the local expert on the trails of your region.

You already have some idea of the type of terrain you like. Mountain trails may turn you on, or long-distance desert treks may be your notion of a good time. You have a lot of delightful choices, and you can enjoy all of them. So for your tour of the Southwest's national parks and monuments, decide on the kind of area you'd like to explore.

Don't limit yourself to the better-known parks and monuments, or to just one kind of area. Most of us think of mountains when we plan an outdoor trip; there are dozens of other landscapes we ignore. Take time to find out about as many of them as you can, and sample them as often as you like. You may be surprised at what you'll find by visiting the smaller parks and monuments. They're usually less crowded, and always as delightful in their own way as the Grand Canyons, the Yosemites and the Yellowstones. All of them, even the smallest, are truly "crown jewels".

GETTING INFORMATION

When you've tentatively selected an area, learn all you can about it. The better you understand a landscape, the more you'll like it. Nearly every city has a good public library, and most cities have a community college or university whose library is stocked with good books. Take advantage of your local public and college libraries. The librarians will take you under their wing if you express the slightest interest in using their facility, and they can order even obscure titles through the interlibrary loan system.

Read not only any guide-books you can find about your area, but other books and articles about similar regions and landscapes as well. Find out what you can about the park or monument's wildlife, its vegetation, weather, geology and history. If possible, talk to people who have been there — most Senior hikers like to share information about their trips. You will, too, once you get to know an area. Once you've traveled through it and have begun to understand its fascination, you're on your way to becoming an expert. Just remember, the more you know about an area, the better you'll like it when you finally get there.

Yet another good source of information about national parks and monuments are the directors of your local college's or public school's outdoor education programs. The people in charge of these are usually glad to give hints and information to Seniors. In fact, you may find that the instructor will not only have been there, he may have maps and other information he's willing to share. Generally, these are knowledgeable people, well worth cultivating. You might even want to take an outdoor education course or a field trip. You'll find they're both enjoyable and informative.

If there's a local chapter of a national conservation or outdoor club in your city, you're in luck — you'll never lack for companions on the trail. The Audubon Society, the Sierra Club and a score of other organizations offer hikes of every variety, from half-day hikes to extended overnighters. In addition, the leaders of the hikes are almost universally well-versed in outdoor skills. Not only will you pick up valuable information for your own use, you'll be supporting some vital environmental work.

Probably the best source of information, of course, is the national park or monument itself. There's a wealth of written information about every national park and monument. Even the smallest have brochures and other publications concerned with the main attractions of the park. They'll be glad to provide a publications list describing books and pamphlets available at their visitor center.

Generally, a phone call to the park or monument will yield an address to write requesting information. Describe the trip you have in mind, and they'll respond with information about your destination. Often they'll send "give away" maps (detailed enough for you to use in planning your hikes), as well as other general information you'll find useful. They'll have information on any hazards you might encounter, wildlife, unusual attractions, and so on. They'll also include their list of publications about the park or monument, with directions for ordering.

Here's something to remember when you approach any of the national parks and monuments about a trip: officers of the National Park Service are public servants in the very best sense of the term. I've always been impressed by the courtesy they extend, even when I've asked dumb questions and taken up too much of their time. I've found National Park Service employees to be helpful and courteous, interested in helping a park visitor get all the enjoyment, inspiration and insight a visit to a national park or monument can bring.

A WORD ABOUT MAPS

By the time you've gone this far in your planning, you'll want to give some thought to locating more detailed maps for your area. Luckily, this too is easy. The national park or monument probably sent you either a sketchy map of the area or a list of the detailed topographic maps covering it. Since you'll want maps for nearly any outdoor trip, I suggest you use either a good guide-book to the park or monument or the US Geological Survey's topographical maps. You don't have to be an expert in orienteering to find either of these helpful.

The USGS issues topographic maps for nearly all areas of the nation, including each national park. If you can't find the topographic maps you need at local mountaineering and outdoor sports shops, you can order the USGS's free index showing the maps they have available. Nearly all the national parks and monuments have a one-sheet USGS topographic map covering the entire park or monument. The USGS can also can send you explanations of the symbols used on topographic maps. For areas east of the Mississippi, write: Distribution Branch, USGS, 1200 Eads Street, Arlington, Virginia 22202. If you need maps for areas west of the Mississippi, write: Distribution Branch, USGS, Federal Center, Denver, Colorado 80225.

Topographic maps are detailed representations of the terrain, giving elevation, distance, direction and a wealth of other information. Several sizes or scales of maps are used: the 7.5-minute series has a scale of 1:24000, or about one inch of map for each 2000 feet of actual terrain. These are the most detailed maps commonly available. The 15-minute series has a scale of 1:62500, or about one inch to one mile on the ground. Two other sizes of map are used: the 1:125000 series and the 1:250000 series. On these, the 1:125000 series has one inch representing just under two miles, and the 1:250000 series has one inch equalling almost four miles.

The larger-scale maps, the 7.5 and 15-minute series, are much easier to read, but they cover less territory. You'll need several to show all the area you'll be traveling through (unless your map covers the entire park or monument). Get as many as you need to cover your route, or else find and use a good guidebook.

For areas covered by more than one map or quadrangle (as each area defined by latitude and longitude is termed), you'll need a whole group of maps. Don't be overwhelmed — you'll quickly learn how to use the maps and discover that they not only help you find your way, but show you in great detail the country you're traveling through. You'll be able to get a much better overview of the area and a much better understanding of the park or monument's landscape.

Here's a bit of information that may save you hours of frustration: always check the date of publication and revision date of your topographic map or guide-book. Often there will have been changes in the area since the map or guide-book was published. Trails, for instance, may have been rerouted or may have disappeared over the years. Man-made objects, especially, may have changed. Cabins do fall, and the works of man don't last forever. Don't expect all of man's artifacts to stay put. Terrain, thank goodness, tends to stay in one place, so use the location of terrain features as the ultimate check of your map-reading skills. You may not be lost after all.

If you're very lucky, someone may have published a good guide-book to your national park or monument. Some guide-books are very, very good — well worth the money. Others, though, may be either outdated or misleading. Rather than depend on a poor guide-book, spend the time necessary to learn enough about your area to have a sense of whether or not a particular guide-book is worthwhile. The very best guide-books will have clear and accurate maps or descriptions, give some idea of the natural and human history of the region, and are valuable additions to your outdoor library.

Remember, though, if there's a guide-book for your destination, you may find that you've chosen a popular area. Dozens or hundreds of outdoor travelers may have been attracted to a place simply because it's been publicized. Better, I think, to forge your own route and take responsibility for the success of your own trip. (Then, when you return, you can write a guide-book of your own — unless you want to keep the best places for your own secret hideaway.)

3

SELECTING A TRAIL

Once you've narrowed your destination to a particular national park or monument, it's time to select the trails or routes that suit you best. Whatever your choice, it should reflect your own interests, the time you have available, and your own physical condition.

Most Senior hikers will try to cover too much country in too little time. Don't overdo it, and don't fall into the trap of "I have to see it all right now". With a little planning your visit can be leisurely, and you can still hike all the trails that interest you. Remember, too, that if you enjoy your trip to a particular park or monument, you'll want to return for another visit. Take it easy on yourself — you'll increase your pleasure and decrease your stress, and you'll have a good excuse for coming back.

After all, you've probably had to rush through too many pleasant experiences in your younger years, wishing there were enough time to enjoy them fully. Now you have the opportunity to savor your hard-won freedom from clocks and calendars. Take as long as you want — at last, Time has become your ally. Besides, if you hike the trail slowly and at your own pace, you'll soon find that you're seeing things others miss, and enjoying experiences that simply aren't possible to those on a rigid timetable. Naturally, if you find that you've missed seeing part of the park or monument, you can always make another visit.

CHOOSE A TRAIL THAT SATISFIES YOUR OWN INTERESTS

Most of the time the Senior hiker will be looking for an interesting experience — and that's the best reason a Senior can have for day-hiking in a particular national park or monument. Select your route to be as strenuous or easy as you like; it's your trip, so enjoy it.

You probably already have some national park or monument in mind, and some particular thing that's drawn you to a certain area. It may be fishing, photography, or just wanting to get away from people. Or it could be that you want to see new areas and do new things. Whatever the attraction, let your interests be your guide as you select your route and plan your hiking.

For instance, if photographing the scenery of a national park or monument is your primary interest, you can easily use maps and the written descriptions in guide-books to outline a route that will take you to the most scenic places and allow you to get outstanding photographs.

If you're a photographer, you'll want to plan your itinerary to take advantage of the best times of day for shooting your particular subjects. That means you'll want to arrange your trip so that most subjects are photographed when the light is best, rather than just taking a few shots whenever you happen to get there.

Most subjects photograph best during the hours between sunrise and about 10 am, and again from between about 2 pm and sunset, when the light is warmer and shadows are longer. You won't be able to cover as many miles on the trail as non-photographers, but if you want outstanding photographs, you have to be in the right place with the right light. Keep in mind that not all great photographs are taken when the light is "just right". By ignoring the common wisdom about proper times of day for photography, you may discover that once-in-a-lifetime shot. Take it and be glad you did.

Remember as well that not all the great photographic subjects have to be landscapes. Plan your route so that there's time to find those intriguing close-ups of the smaller things found in the area. They, too, are part of the landscape, but are often overlooked if you're concentrating on the classical peak-and-sunset shots. If you're like most photographers, you won't need any urging to find good subjects — they'll overwhelm your capacity to record them.

As another example of picking trails to suit a particular interest, consider how a confirmed fisherman might go about it. If your objective is to find the best fishing then you'll select your route accordingly, just as a photographer might. Unfortunately, most lakes and streams that are accessable will have a well-worn trail to them and a hard-packed path along the water's edge. Unfortunately, too, the fishing-spot will usually have too much evidence of other fishermen having tried their luck in your particular lake or stream.

By glancing at the map or guidebook and carefully selecting your route, you can often find relatively unfished waters, but it'll sometimes mean going beyond where the casual fisherman stops.

Careful use of topographic maps will help you find lakes and streams that are overlooked by most fishermen. The topographic map will also tell you how high the lake or stream is, how extensive its drainage, and give you other information about the prospects of a good catch. Use the map, and your desire for good fishing will lead you to some of the most memorable sport you've had. Just remember to check with the rangers at the park's visitor center about licenses and fishing regulations.

GETTING AWAY FROM THE CROWDS

If you want to get away from people, the opportunity is available in nearly every national park or monument — if you select your route and your time of visit carefully. Most hikers and other outdoor travelers will tend to concentrate along trails, so plan your route to avoid the most popular corridors as much as possible. Try to hike away from the main attractions and you'll not only see fewer people, you may discover places and things few other Senior hikers have found.

There's a reason some places are called "attractions" — they attract people. To get away from the crowd, plan your route and itinerary so you're at the attraction when everyone else is some other place. As a Senior, you can change the season when you're traveling, or the time of day or the day of the week. If you want to avoid overpopulated campgrounds and crowded trails, do your hiking and camping in midweek rather than on weekends, and by all means avoid holidays. Go somewhere else at those times — be where the crowds aren't.

It's amazing that a place as spectacular as, say, Yosemite Valley can be nearly deserted at certain times. A popular national park may be grossly overcrowded at one season, and nearly vacant a few weeks later. Timing, it seems, is the important thing. To enjoy uncrowded attractions, try to arrange your schedule to avoid crowds. You have the freedom and time to travel, so make it comfortable and enjoyable for yourself.

CHOOSE A TRAIL YOU CAN HANDLE

Most of us are going to select our trail or route by terrain, of course. We want to see the vistas from the highest points, experience the feeling of the true desert, feel the power of an ocean or know the tranquility of a prairie sunrise. We'll pick the landscape we want, and then enjoy it as much as we can. You'll find plenty of trails that fit all the criteria you've established, including miles of trails that suit your own physical condition.

Since landscape or terrain dictates where we go and what we do, it's important to be realistic about what's possible and what isn't. Not all of us are in good enough physical shape to get to the top of the Grand Teton, but most of us can manage an ascent of a somewhat lesser peak, and feel justifiably proud when we stand on the summit. If we're not up for a trek across Death Valley (thanks just the same) we take a less arduous but equally interesting desert hike that will let us feel just as good when we finish. The key is moderation, and understanding what's possible and what isn't. Your own knowledge of your physical condition is the primary consideration.

No matter what you did in your younger years, it's important to understand that being in reasonably good physical shape is desirable. If you're in fairly good health, day-hikes shouldn't be beyond your ability. Of course, before you undertake any strenuous physical activity you should have a good idea of what your body can or can't do — then only a physician's opinion should keep you from undertaking day-hikes. In fact, hiking is good medicine, especially if done leisurely, safely and comfortably. By all means try hiking — it's good for the body (regardless of your age) and a delightful tonic for the mind.

Physical conditioning, by the way, is more than being able to carry a pack for a couple of miles. It includes acclimation to elevation, getting used to different (not better or worse) food and water, and a lot of other things that take time. Your plans, then, should take into account your body's need to adjust to new and different elevations, stresses, and routines. If you don't have time to acclimate, select a route that doesn't require acclimation. You'll have a better time, and your body will thank you for taking it easy at first.

WHAT IF YOUR DREAM TRIP ISN'T POSSIBLE RIGHT NOW?

Suppose, though, you can't find either time or money for that dream outdoor trip. Don't let that stop you from taking day-hikes. You can always find nearby national parks and monuments that offer hiking, backcountry travel and other outdoor activities.

Again, most cities have several organizations concerned about the environment — a chapter of the Sierra Club, a college's outing group, or just a group of people who like the same things you like. Get in touch with them; they'll be glad to have another person interested in their favorite sport. They can point out local areas they know well, and they'll be helpful in getting you started correctly.

Another good source of information about areas within a day's drive of your home are state and local agencies concerned with natural resources. State fish, game and park departments and other agencies under different names may be involved in outdoor recreation. You'll be surprised to find that they have some very attractive areas under their jurisdiction, and that many of them are open to outdoor activities similar to those you're interested in.

Probably the best way to locate nearby destinations is to

cultivate a circle of friends interested in outdoor travel. Sharing tales of outdoor adventures is fun (the more exaggerated the better, usually), and outdoor people make great friends. You'll probably find others in your town who like outdoor travel as much as you. Pick their brains, find their favorite spots, and begin enjoying the outdoors with them. You won't be sorry you did.

Remember, no matter what your age, interests or physical condition, there are trails in the southwestern national parks and monuments that you can handle. With a little thought, a little planning and a few basic items of equipment, you'll soon be ready to hit the trail. And I assure you it'll be one of the safest, most enjoyable and most pleasant experiences of your life.

Bandelier National Monument   (NPS photo)

Organ Pipe Cactus National Monument   (NPS photo)

4

CLOTHING AND BOOTS FOR SENIOR DAY-HIKERS

Not many things are required for day-hiking in the southwestern national parks and monuments — most of the clothing Seniors need can be found lurking in the back of a closet or hidden in a storage box. You'll need only a few basic items: appropriate clothing, suitable boots or other footgear, a day-pack of some sort, a first-aid or emergency kit, a canteen of water and something to snack on. Depending on your interests, you'll probably enjoy taking along a field guide or two, a camera, and even a pair of light-weight binoculars. First, let's look at clothing and boots for the well-dressed Senior hiker.

THE WELL-DRESSED SENIOR HIKER

Take time to assemble the necessary clothing and other gear. You'll use these basic items on hike after hike; before long they'll seem like old friends, always there when you need them.

Most Senior hikers won't have any problem finding suitable clothing for their day-hikes. Clothing styles range from specially-designed jackets and parkas to well-used and comfortable fugitives from the trash-bin. Your spouse may deplore your favorite old sweater, but it might be just the thing for a cool day on the trail.

However it looks and whatever it costs, clothing for the trail should serve three important functions — it should protect you, insulate you, and above all it should be comfortable. If an item doesn't do all three, you'll not only find that your hikes aren't as enjoyable as they should be, they may be downright dangerous.

The garments you wear on the trail must provide good protection from the environment. They should be able to shrug off most thorns and stickers without ripping or tearing, and they should be sturdy enough of offer some protection from scrapes and scratches if you slip and fall.

Insulation is important, too, whether you're hiking on a cool, moist mountain trail or hiking cross-country in a hot desert. Your clothing is your first line of defense against hypothermia, the excessive loss of body heat, and your best ally in resisting overheating. Insulation, of course, can be added or removed to suit the hiking conditions, but only if you've remembered to bring the correct types of clothing.

Comfort is just as important. For Seniors, this means wearing relatively loose-fitting clothing on the trail. Tight jeans, for instance, are too restrictive for most of us, and even a pull-over jacket that fits fine with a thin shirt under it may require the contortions of an Olympic gymnast when you try to add a wool sweater. Whether you use clothing you already have or buy new garments for the trail, be sure to keep the three functions of trail clothing in mind — protection, insulation and comfort. If it fits these criteria, it's probably right for day-hiking.

Do all these things work on the trail to make your hike safer and more comfortable? Yes, they do — if you learn to take advantage of "layering". Basically, the layering system is simply adding or removing thin layers of clothing as conditions change. If you're too warm you remove a layer, too cool, then add one. If you're hiking on a cool morning, you'll probably start by wearing several layers. As the day warms, you'll remove the layers and stow them in your day-pack. If you stop to rest and become chilly, you'll add a sweater or shirt. By carrying several thinner garments you can add or remove clothing to suit your own body's requirements and the demands of the environment around you.

RECOMMENDED CLOTHING FOR SENIOR DAY-HIKERS

While you can enjoy most day-hikes with ordinary servicable outdoor clothing, hikers have found that some designs and materials work better than others. Experienced Senior hikers have discovered combinations that make hiking more comfortable and safer. You don't need to rush out and buy all new clothing and equipment if what you already have meets the requirements of protection, insulation and comfort. As you gain more experience, though, you may want to replace your present gear with items specifically designed for safe, comfortable hiking. The information below can help you decide if what you have is adequate for the hikes you'll be taking.

PARKAS

No matter where you're hiking, be it desert or mountain, you'll need protection for the upper body. The function of a parka is to protect you from wet and windy conditions —

conditions which rob the body of heat and may lead to chilling or even hypothermia.

A good parka offers at least minimal protection from water penetration. The very best, made of the super-fabric Gore-Tex, BION II or another "micropore" fabric, protects as well as most heavily-coated waterproof parkas but still allows body moisture to escape — thus keeping perspiration from soaking your clothes from the inside. All well-designed parkas will give good protection from wind penetration as well. And if you're protected from wind and wetness, hypothermia and over-chilling are nearly impossible. The things to look for in a parka, then, are the protection it offers from penetration of wind and water, and whether or not it allows your own body moisture to escape.

A parka doesn't have much insulation — its function is to protect underlying garments. Most parks have a hood to protect the head from excessive heat loss, as well as adjustable sleeves which can be opened for cooling or closed to prevent wind and water penetration. Most also feature a drawstring at the waist, again to protect against drafts and the resulting heat loss.

Seniors should look for a parka or other outer jacket that's roomy enough to cover an extra sweater and a wool shirt without making you go through contortions when you add or remove layers. For all practical purposes, that means pull-over or anorak styles are out. They're just too binding for most of us to wear comfortably.

Look for a parka with good water-repellent or water-proof characteristics, but one that's designed so you can ventilate body moisture. As you exercise, body moisture must be vented either through the fabric of your clothing or through neck, sleeve, and waist openings. If it isn't, you're likely to soak your clothing from the inside — just as bad as soaking it from the outside.

If a hood bothers you look for a design that either has a roll-up hood or lacks a hood altogether. Just remember to carry a hat.

PANTS

Pants serve the Senior mainly for protection; they're your first line of defense against sunburn, poison ivy, stickers and thorns, and even insect bites. As long as the pants are roomy and comfortable, they'll be fine for all but the worst conditions.

You'll probably want to avoid cotton jeans — they tend to be hot in hot weather and cold in cold weather. In addition, cotton tends to wick moisture, so if the cuffs of your jeans get wet you can count on the moisture traveling up your leg, cooling you more than you might want. In addition, most jeans are cut fairly tight in the crotch and rump. Some Seniors find this most uncomfortable, especially when actively hiking.

Much as cotton jeans have going against them, I usually hike in worn-out Levis, and so will you. Jeans are relatively inexpensive, and you probably already have several pairs. They're fine on most trails, but beware of their pitfalls.

You may find pants of polyester-cotton-spandex more comfortable. They tend to have more give than most other types of trousers and they're durable, inexpensive, and look good. The six-pocket design ("trail pants") are great for Seniors, and look sharp. I've never had occassion to use all the pockets but maybe you will.

In wet conditions you'll need more protection and insulation than cotton or cotton-blend pants will give. In wet and chilly country, you'll want wool or wool-blend pants.

Spend as much or as little as you want for these. You can spend up to $100 for tightly-woven hard-finish whipcord wool trousers, or less than $5 for wool suit-pants from a thrift store. Not as stylish, perhaps, but the price is right.

SWEATERS AND SHIRTS

Layering is the key to providing proper insulation, and sweaters and shirts provide the insulating layers. Again, you don't have to spend much money to be adequately outfitted. Any wool sweater will do as long as it's roomy enough to wear over a heavy shirt.

If you want the finest, go either with an all-wool sweater or one of the newer synthetic pile, fleece or bunting sweaters. These weigh less than wool, are easily washed and quickly dried, and have the advantage of not itching as wool sometimes does.

Whether wool or synthetic, the sweater should be easy to put on and remove. Some Seniors like the pull-over styles, while others swear by the cardigan or zip-front design. No matter which type you prefer, make sure it's big enough to be easy to wear and simple to remove.

Under the sweater goes a shirt. I prefer cotton for hot desert hikes, and demand wool for hikes in cooler country (or country that has the potential for turning cool). Most Senior hikers will want long sleeves for protection from sunburn and insect bites. The sleeves can always be rolled if you like the feel of cool breezes against your skin.

SOCKS

If you wear the right socks, they'll provide insulation (important for keeping heat out as well as in), padding, and some protection from blisters.

Most hikers prefer wool or wool-blend socks, often with a thinner cotton or cotton-blend inner sock. Use the sock or sock combination that feels best to you, and the one that you think will help prevent blisters. I know some Seniors who wear only a thin pair of cotton socks and get along fine. I know others, though, who get blisters just thinking about hiking in less than two pairs of heavy wool stockings. It's your choice, and it'll depend on your boots and the tenderness of your feet.

Always carry a spare set of socks, and don't be afraid to stop and change socks or to vary the combination. It's much better to experiment a bit than suffer blisters or sore feet. And remember, lumps or folds in the socks invite blisters, just as do holes, so make sure the socks are smooth and in good shape. Blisters will keep you off the trail and make your life miserable — don't take a chance with them.

UNDERGARMENTS

Wear whatever seems most comfortable for you, but if you're carrying a day-pack, avoid anything that has either very narrow or very thick straps over the shoulders. The pack straps will chafe against any seam or thick spot and might irritate the skin or bruise the underlying muscle tissue.

RAINGEAR AND WINDGEAR

Sooner or later you'll be caught on the trail in wet and windy condtions. Even in the desert afternoon, thundershowers can soak a hiker and cool him to the point of hypothermia. Protection from wind and moisture are essential safety considerations — not to be forgotten at any time.

If your parka is water-proof (either coated or of a micropore fabric like Gore-Tex or BION II) you're well-protected. If not, you'll need a protective garment of some sort. Some hikers carry a poncho — essentially a walking tarp — for rainy spells. Ponchos are fine for sitting around in, but nearly useless when the wind comes up as it always does. Some Seniors like to carry a light-weight waterproof jacket of coated nylon or even plastic to slip on. These aren't very durable, but certainly do the job.

Whatever you use, remember that body moisture can soak your insulation quickly and completely. Your wind and rain gear should allow you to ventilate or otherwise get rid of body moisture while still protecting you from rain and wind.

Whether your wind and rain protection is a garment of super-fabric, coated material or plastic, how and when you use it depends on your judgement. Always remember to carry it on the trail — it's of no use if you don't have it.

BETWEEN YOU AND THE TRAIL — BOOTS AND FOOTGEAR

If there's one item of equipment that'll make or break your day-hike, it's your footwear. Boots protect the foot, give traction when it's needed, insulate the foot from heat and cold, and still can be as comfortable as your favorite slippers. Boots should do all these things, but sometimes they don't.

There are dozens of different types of hiking boots, from the heavy, stiff mountaineering or "heavy-hiking" boot to light-weight cousins of the running shoe. Any of them can get you down the trail, but some will do it better and more comfortably than others.

Most Senior hikers are well-advised to stay away from the heavy-hiking or mountaineering boot. These are designed for those who often hike cross-country, carry heavy loads, and do at least some scrambling or climbing. Most of us will never need the protection and insulation given by such a heavy boot.

More in line with the needs of Senior hikers are medium-weight hiking boots, which have a fair degree of stiffness (but are much more flexible than the heavy-hikers), provide adequate insulation for most conditions, give good traction, and have fine durability. If you carry a fairly light load, hike moist, rocky or wet trails, travel cross-country occassionally, or hike in fairly snowy conditions this is usually the boot of choice.

Most Seniors, though, will be more comfortable in a still lighter boot. The trail shoe, light-hiker, light-weight hiking boot or light-weight trail boot is designed for lighter loads and better trails. Best of all, the boot is flexible and a joy to wear. Comfort, however, means giving up some of the protection and insulation of a heavier boot. This is the boot to buy unless you absolutely require a heavier boot to stand up to your particular choice of trails.

Light-weight hiking boots can be found with uppers of either leather or fabric. I don't think the material used in the uppers should be of too much concern unless you'll be doing a lot of hiking in wet conditions. For wet, soppy trails you'll want an upper which can be water-proofed for added protection from moisture. Even under the wettest conditions, though, fabric uppers containing a layer of Gore-Tex or another micropore fabric do the job adequately. The choice is yours, and depends on the kinds of hiking you'll be doing.

There's some question about whether or not you really need a hiking boot at all. Some hikers get along fine wearing sneakers or running shoes, some do all right with heavier work-boots and some even use street shoes. I don't think it really matters, as long as your footwear is comfortable, offers at least minimal protection and good traction on the trail. A word of caution, though — sore feet and blisters ruin hikes, and so do sprained ankles. Good footwear is a must for Senior hikers — this is one item you can't afford to stint on.

BUYING BOOTS

If you're in the market for boots, be prepared to spend time finding the right boot, getting the right size, and trying them out. Buying boots always seems to take all afternoon, but the time spent will be worth it when you're on the trail in a pair of comfortable, correctly-fitting boots.

Take along a couple pairs of socks when shopping for boots — the combination of socks you'll be wearing on the trail. Try on the boots wearing the sock combination, and carefully check the boot's length. The best way to do this is to push your toe to the front of the unlaced boot, then stick your index finger behind your heel. If your toes don't bump the end of the boot when your finger is snugly inserted at the heel, the size is probably about right.

Next lace the boots and stand on your toes or otherwise try to move your foot forward in the boot. You're close to a good fit if your toes still don't touch the end of the boot. Width is best determined, I think, by your subjective judgement of how the boot feels on your own foot. If either length or width feels wrong, try another pair or vary your sock combination (even to the extent of changing the combination from foot to foot). Keep experimenting until you think you've found the right pair for you.

You're not quite through yet. Wear the boots around the store for a while, trying them out. If there's any question about the fit, try other boots until you're satisfied they're comfortable enough for years of wear. Take your time —

it's much better to discover poorly-fitting boots in the shop than on the trail.

Like other Seniors, you may have extraordinary feet. Bone spurs, bunions, altered bone placement, fallen arches — all may require extra care in fitting a boot to your foot. If you've chosen a leather boot rather than boots made with fabric uppers, the leather can be stretched carefully to conform to bunions or bone spurs. (Some shoe stores can do this, or can recommend a shop having the right equipment for stretching specific areas of the boot.) Fallen arches, displaced bones and other problems may require special insoles, arch supports, heel lifts or other appliances. If your feet continue to give you problems, consult a physician or podiatrist for professional advice. They can suggest alternatives and get you on the trail in light-footed comfort.

Once you've purchased a pair of comfortable hiking boots, the next step is to break them in. There are dozens of tales about the proper way to break in boots, ranging from advice to wade a stream in them to soaking your new boots in various questionable liquids. But don't do more than wear your new boots around the house for a few days. Leather stretchs only slightly, and won't do much more than conform to your foot. Walking a few miles in new boots are all the breaking-in that's required — if you bought flexible, well-fitting boots. That's all there is to it.

Sweaters, parkas, raingear, pants, boots — all part of the well-dressed Senior hiker's wardrobe. Sounds like a lot of things to buy and a lot of choices to make. Don't despair, though, if you can't rush out and buy all new gear. Find a pair of old comfortable shoes with good traction, an adequate jacket and sweater and something to keep the wind and rain from getting to you — then you're ready for the trail. As you find you need specialized equipment, you can add it to your wardrobe. If your clothing and footgear serve the three functions of protection, insulation, and comfort you're ready for a day-hike.

Bandelier National Monument   (NPS photo)

5

HIKING HARDWARE — SAFE AND EASY

Once the question of clothing and footgear is settled you're nearly ready for the trail. All that remains is to decide where to leave the car, what to take with you, and how to carry it all.

It used to be that day-hiking was a fairly spartan and uncomfortable pastime — a hiker would stuff his pockets with an apple, a hunk of cheese and a pocketknife, sling a camera over his shoulder and jam a birdbook in his back pocket. With those few things he was set for a day on the trail. Extra clothing, if any, was tied around the waist in a sort of cumberbund. Binoculars, field guides, first-aid supplies and emergency kits were either unknown or left behind. If the hiker were extra cautious, he'd find room for a map and a compass. No wonder the trails were nearly deserted; hiking, even day-hiking, was seen as a masochistic sport.

Those days are long gone, thanks to the development of new lightweight daypacks, specially-designed clothing, better boots, smaller cameras and even featherweight binoculars. Now the Senior day-hiker can travel light and still have all the gear necessary for a safe, comfortable and educational outing. All it takes is a little care and forethought in selecting what you take and how you carry it.

You can be comfortable in the knowledge that your car or camper is safe, and that you have the clothing, first-aid supplies and emergency gear needed to meet nearly any situation. With what you have on your back, you can be as safe and well-protected as you would be in your own home.

YOU CAN TAKE IT WITH YOU — DAYPACKS AND BELTPACKS

You'll want to carry some bulky items on your day-hike — sweaters, water and food, a first-aid and emergency kit, a camera, and perhaps even field-guides and binoculars. You'll be carrying gear to provide for your safety and comfort, as well as items to pursue your particular interests. You'll need either a daypack or a beltpack roomy enough to hold it all. But don't panic — the total weight of all the gear you'll usually need on a day-hike will be less than ten pounds or so, and today's pack designs will make even that light load comfortable and easy to carry.

There are two main designs of packs suitable for Senior day-hikers. The first is the old reliable daypack, essentially a cloth sack fitted with shoulder straps, and often with external pockets and a waistband or other arrangement which prevents the pack from swaying as you move along the trail. The second design, the beltpack, is really nothing more than a large pocket which straps around your waist. Naturally both designs have been refined and modified until there are countless varieties of each. You'll want to examine several beltpacks and daypacks before deciding which is best for you.

Most Seniors find a daypack more comfortable than a beltpack. A daypack puts more weight on the shoulders (unless fitted with a hipbelt of some sort) but is easier to put on and take off. A beltpack straps around the waist, putting most of the weight and pressure on the abdomen. Unless the load is very light, many Seniors will find this restrictive and uncomfortable.

A good daypack will have a fairly large capacity (about the size of a large grocery sack) and will have at least two outside pockets. I find, as do most Senior day-hikers, that an internal frame built into the pack is more comfortable than a floppy frameless bag. When it's filled to capacity, carrying a frameless daypack is a lot like walking around with a bowling ball strapped to your shoulders. In addition to supporting the load, the frame greatly reduces the chances that sharp objects in the bag will dig into your back — an uncomfortable nuisance that can ruin any hike.

Some daypacks have a built-in hip belt which places much of the pack's weight on the hips, reducing the pull on the shoulders. Whether your pack has a hip belt or not, well-padded shoulder straps are a must, and they should be easily adjustable in length.

Other important things to look for when buying a daypack are a pocket built into the top flap, plastic zippers for top and side pockets, and a design that's convenient to carry and easy to load. Look, too, at the arrangement of the frame or the back padding, and avoid daypacks that don't put anything soft between you and the load.

If you find the idea of carrying a daypack less than thrilling, or if you habitually suffer from sore shoulders, you may want to try a beltpack. A beltpack is more comfortable for some Seniors, although the capacity of a beltpack is usually much smaller, and some Seniors are bothered by any restriction at all around the waist. If you're worried about carrying too much weight on your shoulders, though, you might try to find a large-volume beltpack. I've discovered that no matter how carefully I load it, there's always something that won't fit. You may be a more careful packer than I — if so, a beltpack may be the way to go.

WHAT TO CARRY ON THE TRAIL

Senior day-hikers can easily carry all the items necessary to insure their comfort, safety and enjoyment. Common sense dictates that you always have food, water, a first-aid and emergency kit, and extra clothing with you. Enjoyment suggests a few other items as well.

Cameras, for instance, are essential items in southwestern national parks and monuments. Today's cameras are lightweight, easy to load and use, and rugged enough to stand up to the jolts and bumps of a day-hike. You'll want to relive your trip, and there's no better way than looking at your own photographs. Just be sure to take enough film, an extra battery (if your camera requires batteries at all) and know how to use your camera and film. This is especially important if your camera has adjustable focus, exposure times, apertures or changeable lenses.

In addition to a camera, I like to take a lightweight pair of binoculars on my day-hikes. They're great for scanning the landscape for wildlife, for birdwatching, for finding trails in the distance, and for just gazing through while I daydream. I like the small, palm-size binoculars with rubber eye-cups. If you wear glasses, you'll want the type with rubber roll-up eye-cups.

Your knowledge of the wilderness will be increased if you know what's around you. Part of the delight of being on the trail in a national park or monument is the assurance of finding plants and animals in their natural habitat. Many

Seniors like to carry a field-guide identifying plants and animals in their particular national park or monument. Every park or monument will have field-guides and natural history books in the park's visitor center. Seniors like to learn new things and understand their world — they find that the extra weight of a field-guide is offset by the enjoyment it brings to their hike. You don't have to carry a complete library, but by all means take a book on the things you're interested in.

FOOD AND DRINK ON THE TRAIL

Some, I think, hike as an excuse for dining well. Others eat practically nothing, existing on stored energy. In my opinion, both are missing something. You should eat well before, during, and after the hike. You'll be using energy that has to be maintained and replaced by the food you consume.

A lot of hikers start with a good breakfast and continue eating throughout the day, making lunch a moving feast. Others like to nibble a bit at midmorning, have a definite lunch and then nibble more in the afternoon. I don't think it makes much difference as long as your energy reserves are maintained.

For most day-hikers lunch will be the only meal actually eaten on the trail. Nearly any menu will do — fruit, crackers, sardines, cheese — whatever you enjoy. Light snacks before and after lunch are delightful, too, and help maintain energy and thus your enjoyment of the hike. Don't worry about taking too much food — you can always carry it back to camp, and it might come in handy if there were an emergency.

Of course, you'll always want to carry plenty of fresh water. Some Seniors enjoy canned fruit juices or soft drinks on the trail — these (unless they're diet drinks) also provide a welcome source of high-energy, easily digested sugar, just the thing to help you over that late-afternoon slump. Gatorade and Gookinaid ERG are also popular with Senior hikers. These drinks contain sodium, magnesium and calcium salts which help replace electrolytes lost through sweating. If you often suffer from leg cramps while hiking try one of these drinks — they may help more than salt tablets.

Remember, of course, that you'll carry out all the pop cans, candy wrappers, banana peels and other left-overs. Not even organic materials should be left behind — they simply won't return to nature. If you packed it in, be doubly sure you pack it out.

BE PREPARED — SOME THINGS TO ALWAYS TAKE

Experience has proven that some items should be carried by Seniors on any day-hike. Most Seniors won't ever need these essential items — but they should always be in your pack. The essential items don't weigh much and don't take up much room, but they may mean the difference between an interesting experience and a tragedy. Always carry them.

EXTRA CLOTHING

Always have more clothing in the pack than you think you'll need. The archives of rescue organizations are filled with stories of hikers who set off on a sunny morning and were unprepared when the weather changed suddenly. Somewhere in the bottom of your pack should be a wind-proof and water-proof jacket or parka — even on desert hikes. Of course, in wetter, cooler country you should have at least a wool sweater or a garment that stays warm when wet (pile, fleece, or bunting). In addition, carry a space-blanket, a thin, nearly weightless sheet of plastic-coated mylar which not only protects you from rain and wind but reflects body heat back onto you where it'll do some good. Remember, the wetter and windier the conditions, the more extra clothing you should have in reserve (a good argument for using a large-capacity daypack).

EXTRA FOOD AND WATER

Just as extra clothing conserves energy, extra food can replenish your energy supply in an emergency. I've carried a bar of mince-meat pie filling, on the theory that it keeps nearly forever and won't be tempting until I really need it. You, too, should stow some high-energy but light-weight rations in the pack, hidden for the day when you'll need some quick energy. If you don't like mince-meat pie, carry at least a couple candy bars or, better yet, mint cake — hard to find, but tasty and it lasts forever. Make sure, too, that your canteen is filled. Don't count on finding pure water anywhere in the backcountry of our southwestern national parks and monuments. Carry water of your own.

KNIFE

You don't need an axe, saw, bayonet or machete on the trail, but you do need a good pocketknife. Probably the most useful and durable are the Swiss Army knives — they're rustless, and even the simplest have several useful tools. Don't get carried away by all the gadgets on the more elaborate models; get the type with one or two blades, screwdrivers and a can-opener — they're all most of us will ever need.

FIRE STARTER AND LIGHTER

On the off-chance you'll need to start a fire, carry a butane lighter in your emergency kit. Tape the wheel and valve with a bit of electrician's tape if you worry about gas escaping, or better yet leave the lighter in it's display packaging. The time-tested alternative, of course, is to carry matches, either waterproofed or in a water-proof container. I prefer the butane lighter — I know it'll work every time. It's good advice, too, to practice starting a fire before you hit the trail — then you'll know you can get a fire going under nearly any condition.

FLASHLIGHT

If you've ever stumbled around in the darkness of a wilderness night, you already know that a good flashlight is a must. Even the simplest will light a trail well enough for you to travel slowly (best not to travel at all after dark; it's better to pace yourself so you don't get caught by darkness). Flashlights tend not to work when they're needed, so carry extra batteries and an extra bulb, and test the light occassionally. I prefer the small, featherweight Mallory AA Compact Light, although there are many other rugged types available. To prevent wearing out the batteries, tape the switch off or reverse one of the batteries when the flashlight isn't being used.

WHISTLE

The human voice doesn't carry well in the wilderness, and yelling takes energy that could be better used for other things. Carry a police whistle, and use it if you have to signal others in an emergency.

MAP AND COMPASS

Although you may not be an expert in the use of map and compass, you may be able to read a map well enough to avoid losing the trail or becoming confused. Even a simple map may be helpful, and they're easily read on the trail. A simple compass, too, can be quite useful — just remember to trust it, as you will when you gain confidence in its use.

SUNGLASSES AND SUNSCREEN

These are essential items on even cloudy days. Seniors often find their skin more sensitive to burning than it once was — and a sunburn can not only be irritating and painful, it can deplete the electrolytes your body needs to function efficiently. The best sunburn preventive is to cover exposed skin with clothing, but that won't always be possible or comfortable. Next best is to use a good brand of sunscreen or sunblock until you become used to the sun. If you want to develop a healthy tan, limit your exposure to a few hours at a time, gradually increasing exposure as your skin becomes conditioned. No matter how careful you are, though, some sensitive areas may still burn. Cover those with a good grade of sunblock.

Sunglasses are needed, too, since your eyes can be damaged by overexposure to intense solar radiation. Plastic lenses, especially the type used with clip-on sunglasses, don't filter infrared radiation and barely filter ultraviolet. If at all possible, use gray-green glass lenses — these don't greatly alter the color of visible light but do filter both infrared and ultraviolet rays. If you wear prescription glasses, you may want your optician to make up a pair of sunglasses to your prescription. The cost will be worth it in increased comfort.

FIRST-AID AND EMERGENCY KIT

You should also carry a minimal first-aid and emergency kit. It should contain at least the following items:

Band-aids — half a dozen, for minor cuts and scrapes

Gauze pads — half a dozen, for deeper, bleeding cuts or extensive scrapes

Adhesive tape — small roll, for holding bandages, taping sprains, covering blisters

Aspirin — for pain and fever

Small needle — for draining blisters and digging out splinters

Moleskin — for covering blisters and "hot-spots"

Salt tablets or rock salt — a few tablets or a few grains of rock salt for use when sweating or exercising heavily (if you're limiting your salt intake, check with your physician for a substitute)

Prescription medications — as per your physician's directions; carry more than enough

Sportsman's space blanket — to conserve body heat in case of chilling, shock or hypothermia

The items listed above should be sufficient for most day-hikes; naturally, if your hike is in more rugged country or if you have some specific ailment that requires attention, you'll want to carry a more extensive first-aid and emergency kit.

Since you'll not be using the essentials or the first-aid and emergency kit continually (or never, with luck) you can stow the items in a small stuff sack or other container. I keep emergency items and first-aid gear in a large cloth wallet, with plastic bags wrapped around anything that might be damaged by water, keeping out only those items I use frequently — sunglasses, sunscreen, pocket knife and so on.

GETTING TO THE TRAILHEAD — SAFE DRIVING

Most Seniors drive to their national park or monument, rather than taking public transportation. This is unfortunate from the standpoint of pollution, overcrowding and stress, but it's a fact of life. Most parks and monuments in the Southwest are relatively isolated, and only reached by automobile.

Distances in the Southwest are long, and towns are few. Automobile travel is quite safe, of course, but there are a few things you can do to make your trip pleasant and trouble-free.

First, always make sure your car is in good mechanical condition. Check the fuel, oil, and water levels frequently — running out of gas is not only embarassing, it's inconvenient and stressful.

Experienced southwestern travelers carry at least a minimal automobile emergency kit with them. You can put one together for a few dollars — well-spent money, since it can save both time and cash. Here's what I carry:

Nylon tow-strap — for pulling vehicles out of sand or back onto the road

Assorted small tools — pliers, screwdrivers, a short length of electrical wire and a few small wrenches will work wonders for minor problems

Electrical tape and duct tape — for minor repairs to electrical wires and for holding parts in place

Fuses — of the sizes for your particular auto

Jumper cables — for starting reluctant engines; make sure you know how to use them

Fuel can and fuel — several gallons in an absolutely leakproof container

Oil — a couple cans of multigrade oil can be a godsend

Water — I carry about five gallons for personal consumption, just in case I get stuck somewhere

Extra food and drink — a couple cans of fruit juice and some nonperishible foods, again just in case

Blankets — southwestern nights get chilly, especially if you're stuck at high elevation

Yes, I carry all this stuff, and no, I've never had to use most of it. But it's like a first-aid kit; you can forget it until it's needed — then it's indispensable.

AT THE TRAILHEAD — SAFE PARKING

Before you leave your car at the trailhead, make sure all valuables are well-hidden, preferably locked in the trunk. Cameras, recorders, binoculars, even sleeping bags and other camping gear are too tempting to be left in view. Don't make yourself or your car an easy target by leaving a note indicating how long you'll be gone — that'll tell a thief how much time he has to make his getaway.

If you have a backcountry permit, always park at the trailhead indicated on it. The rangers will check on your vehicle periodically, discouraging thieves and vandals. If you didn't get a backcountry permit, park in the turnoff or parking area nearest the trailhead, and well off the roadway. Rangers patrol all the roads, and they'll keep an eye on your car while you're on the trail.

If your car should be vandalized or disturbed in any way, be sure to inform the rangers. Information you give may lead to the arrest of vandals or thieves, saving other park visitors from their predations.

EQUIPMENT LIST FOR SENIOR DAY-HIKES

This checklist gives the minimal gear, clothing and equipment you'll need for a day-hike during mild weather and under good conditions. Add or delete items to suit your particular hike — but be cautious about what you leave behind. Remember that conditions can change quickly in the backcountry. Better to have too much clothing, gear, food and water rather than too little.

☐ Boots
☐ Socks
☐ Underwear
☐ Wool shirt
☐ Wool, pile, bunting, or fleece sweater
☐ Pants
☐ Windproof and rainproof parka
☐ Hat
☐ Daypack
☐ Water in canteen
☐ Food
☐ Sunglasses
☐ Sunscreen
☐ Toilet paper
☐ Knife
☐ Butane lighter
☐ Flashlight
☐ Map and compass
☐ Whistle
☐ Insect repellent
☐ First-aid and emergency kit

☐ Camera, film, camera battery, lenses
☐ Binoculars and field guides

With these items, you should be well-prepared for your day-hikes in the southwestern parks and monuments — hikes that will be safe, comfortable and enjoyable.

Death Valley National Monument   (NPS photo)

6

SPECIAL CONSIDERATIONS FOR SENIORS

No matter what their age or physical condition, Seniors can enjoy safe and comfortable day-hikes in the southwestern national parks and monuments. All it takes is a little extra planning, some common sense about the kinds of trails to take, and the wisdom to develop the right attitude. There are a few special considerations Seniors will want to take into account, though.

Some Seniors discover that they're able to take reasonably long hikes without difficulty. Others, however, are more comfortable if they hike shorter distances. Still others find greater enjoyment hiking only during certain seasons of year, and either confine their day-hiking to those times or follow the seasons by going south in the winter and north with the spring. Yet another group of Senior hikers may not enjoy "peak bagging" — they find themselves more comfortable on better developed, more nearly level trails. Don't worry — whatever your particular interest or level of physical ability, you're sure to find suitable hikes in the southwestern national parks and monuments.

Regardless of the type of trail you choose, you'll find a variety of interesting day-hikes, from level paved rambles to challenging backcountry paths. Sample an assortment of them — I don't think you'll be disappointed. You'll quickly learn to pick trails that suit your ability and desires, and soon find that your physical condition won't hold you back on even the most difficult day-hikes. In fact, the more hiking you do, the more you'll enjoy it. With every mile you'll increase your endurance and satisfaction.

BE PREPARED FOR CHANGING CONDITIONS

Trails in the southwestern national parks and monuments are, by and large, wilderness trails. Man is a visitor there and must conform to the dictates of nature. And nature likes to play by her own rules — one of which is a surprising capacity to change quickly. Senior day-hikers have to be ready to accept changing conditions as part of the cost of enjoying and being part of nature. The cost is easily borne since change is one of the most fascinating aspects of the natural world.

Probably the most variable aspect of the southwest is its weather. A Senior may start his day-hike under bright sunny skies, perhaps notice a few clouds building up when he stops for a lunch break, then find himself in a downpour by midafternoon. A downpour, by the way, accompanied by a chilling wind that drives moisture into the clothes and soaks the body if the Senior isn't ready for rainy and windy conditions. For the Senior who's well-prepared, the storm may be only a minor inconvenience or even a delightful interlude; for the unprepared hiker it can spell disaster.

THE MOST DANGEROUS CONDITION — HYPO-THERMIA WEATHER

Hiking in the southwestern national parks and monuments is usually quite safe and comfortable, but the southwest's changeable weather presents several dangers to the unprepared Senior hiker, the most formidable of which is hypothermia.

No matter what season, you should be aware of the dangers of hypothermia — the excessive loss of body heat — and travel prepared to prevent and treat it. Always have some sort of waterproof raingear with you, and carry at least a light jacket, sweater or wool shirt even in summer. The only exception might be for short hikes in the desert, but even there hypothermia may become a problem, especially if you're caught in a brief but chilling storm. It's much better to anticipate conditions leading to chilling and forestall them by adequate preparation. No matter how well-prepared, though, sooner or later you or a companion will have to recognize and treat the symptoms of hypothermia.

Hypothermia occurs when the body loses heat more rapidly than it can be replaced. The early symptoms include shivering and a general slowing of most of the faculties. Speech, for instance, becomes slowed and slurred, vision may be distorted and the victim may stumble or be less coordinated than usual. This may be followed by listlessness, light-headedness and increased irritability, with sudden changes in mood. All these clues indicate over-chilling or incipient hypothermia.

Hypothermia, at least in its early stages, is easily treated. If you or a companion should become chilled, quickly move to a place out of the wind and try to rewarm the victim as quickly as possible. Replace wet clothes, give him something hot to drink, or even snuggle next to him. The key to treatment is preventing further loss of body-heat. Your quick action may mean the difference between a merely uncomfortable experience and a real disaster.

Naturally, it's much easier to prevent overchilling or hypothermia than to treat it, so anticipate "hypothermia conditions" — wet, cool, and windy weather — by carrying enough clothing and raingear to protect yourself.

OTHER WEATHER-RELATED HAZARDS

Summer storms in the Southwest can bring an added danger, lightning. If caught in a thunderstorm, take some precautions to avoid being struck by electrical discharges. Don't, for instance, stand under a tall tree for protection from a shower, or seek shelter in caves or beneath overhangs. Lightning may sometimes spark across the openings of such shelters, much as electrical discharges cross the gap of a spark plug. Don't be caught between the electrodes. It's better to put on raingear and crouch in a low spot with your arms and legs held close to your body. The storm will soon pass and you can safely continue your hike. If possible, watch the storm — they're fascinating examples of nature's power.

Another, but minor, danger to Senior day-hikers is that of flash-flooding, especially in canyons, gullies, and arroyos. Don't get caught in the bottom of a stream by an unexpected gully-washer. Take time to be aware of the environment around you — if you see a thunderstorm is dropping a lot of rain on the watershed above you, then be alert to the very slight possibility of a flash flood. The chances of being caught in a flash flood are extremely remote, but if you should be surprised by one, simply climb higher on the side wall of the canyon or gully. Don't try to outrun a flash flood; they typically move too fast for you to outdistance. By the way, flash floods are so rare that you might want to report any you witness to a ranger.

Changeable conditions or not, the southwestern national parks and monuments are delightful places for day- hiking. Seniors can choose a variety of trails, from gentle walks to the most challenging of excursions. All of them, easy or difficult, reward the Senior hiker with an intimate glimpse of nature's moods. Common-sense preparations and an unhurried pace will let you hike southwestern trails safely and comfortably regardless of the weather.

TAKE IT EASY

Most of us, when we discover something we like, have a tendancy to become overenthusiastic. You'll enjoy day-hiking; just remember to take your time and savor it to the fullest. Take it easy, especially at first. You have plenty of time — there's no reason to rush down the trail. Instead of seeing how fast you can hike, or how many miles you can put under your boots, hike a little slower and enjoy the scenery. You'll feel better and see a lot more that way. Besides, it'll give you a chance to improve your physical conditioning gradually — especially if you've been leading a relatively sedentary life.

How much should you do in one day? That's a question only you can answer. Some Seniors hike a mile or two and are satisfied; others won't rest until they've reached some goal they've set for themselves. I tend to join the first group. Too many of us have spent our lives meeting challenges, setting goals and competing for prizes — why continue doing that the rest of our lives? Hike at your own pace, be it fast or slow, but take enough time to savor the scenery.

There are four things you might want to consider in deciding how much to do in one day. I call them the "comfort factors". The four comfort factors are time, distance, weather, and interests.

The first comfort factor is the amount of time you have available. If you know you have only a limited time to spend in a park or monument, choose a shorter trail or hike only a section of the route. You'll soon learn your most comfortable pace and be able to estimate how long it'll take to hike a specific trail.

The second comfort factor depends on the distance you want to hike. This is related to your physical condition, the condition of the trail (you'll hike more slowly on a steep or poorly-maintained trail), and how you feel on any particular day. You may feel great, like hiking several miles, or the day may be cloudy and gray and you feel like just a short walk. It doesn't make any difference — do what you feel best doing. You can always come back and hike the rest of a trail on another visit.

Weather is the third comfort factor. It affects our attitude, making us feel like staying in bed when it's gloomy outside, or letting us skip down the trail on a bright sunny day. If you're worried about the weather, or if it seems oppressive, choose something else to do that day. Save your hiking for days when the weather's in your favor. If you're on the trail and the weather changes for the worse, consider turning back, especially if you don't feel prepared for the new conditions. Again, you can always continue the hike another day, when the climate's kinder.

The other comfort factor revolves around your own interests. If you're a photographer, for instance, you'll not cover as many miles as someone with other interests. You'll be too busy taking photographs to spend all your time pounding down the trail. If you're watching for animal tracks or sign, you'll also hike more slowly. Pace yourself to accomodate those interests — they're valid, and they make the difference between an interesting trip and just another section of trail marked off on a map.

Time, distance, weather, interests — the comfort factors. You'll soon learn how to balance them to your own satisfaction. When that day comes, you can consider yourself a true Senior day-hiker.

QUESTIONS FOR YOU AND YOUR PHYSICIAN

Hiking is one of the safest and most beneficial pastimes a Senior can do. It provides safe, healthy exercise at a level that's self-limiting — it's hard to overdo it.

However, to be on the safe side, Seniors who are over-weight, have a history of cardiovascular disease or its symptoms, are recovering from an operation or long illness, or who simply are worried about their health should have a thorough medical examination. That way you can begin day-hiking knowing you're starting with a clean bill of health.

Specifically, most authorities on sports injuries and aging agree that if you either have or have suffered from any of the following conditions, you should consult your physician before starting any new exercise program, be it hiking or another sport:

High blood pressure

Heart disease

Chest problems, including asthma or bronchitis

Arthritis or pains in the joints or back

If you suffer from any of these, your health counselor may caution against overdoing your exercise, but most likely he'll congratulate you on your desire to begin such a safe and healthful sport. Just be sure to take it easy at first, until you're used to the exercise.

Whatever you and your physician decide, take a few common sense precautions on your day-hikes. If you or a companion feel discomfort such as nausea, headache, shortness of breath, pounding in the head, dizziness, trembling or pain in the chest, stop immediately. These symptoms are indications that you or your companion have exceeded the limits of your present level of fitness. These distress signals should wear off shortly — if they don't, you should see your health counselor without delay.

Most Senior hikers have a good sense of their own fitness level and abilities; they'll never be bothered by the distress signals mentioned above. In fact, nearly all Seniors find that the more they hike (or get any other reasonable exercise) the better they feel. You will too, I think, especially as you learn to monitor your own physical condition and adjust your hiking activities to how you're feeling.

TRAIL TECHNIQUES TO INCREASE COMFORT AND SAVE ENERGY

Day-hiking is like any other pastime — the more you do the better you get. You'll quickly learn some tricks that'll save energy and help you have a more enjoyable hike.

By all means, start slowly. Muscles, tendons, ligaments, heart — all need a few moments to reach their efficient best. Try to hike at a slower pace for the first few hundred yards or so. Do that and you'll feel fit all day.

Try, too, to travel lightly, but remember to take all the essential items — first-aid and emergency kit, food, water, extra clothing. Leave behind things you won't need except in an emergency. Somehow packs get heavier toward the end of the day. Be well-equipped, but try not to carry any extra weight.

Pick a comfortable pace, and try to maintain it. Most hikers find they cover more ground if they maintain a steady pace rather than rush ahead, throw down their pack and collapse in a heap, then start the process all over. A slower, steadier pace will actually cover more miles more easily, and even let you carry on a conversation while hiking. You'll reach your destination fresh and relaxed if you take it slow and easy.

Don't be competitive in your hiking. If you feel you need to rest, then halt for a few moments. If possible, stop on the crest of a hill out of the wind, or on a level stretch of trail rather than in the middle of a long uphill climb. Nothing is more disheartening than facing a long grade when you put the pack back on. It'll discourage even the best of us.

I find that it helps as well to slow down on uphill stretches, but to keep going. The ideal pace is one which lets you breath nearly normally — if you're out of breath, you're hiking too fast. Slow down until your pace allows your breathing to return to normal. Your respiration rate is the thing to monitor; if you're out of breath you're trying to hike too fast. Slow down until it returns to a nearly normal rate. That'll save not only energy, but help prevent sore muscles and "hiking burnout" — a condition caused by trying to do too much too fast.

Naturally, it's important to eat and drink regularly while on the trail. Hiking burns lots of calories, and you'll lose more body moisture than if you were just sitting quietly around camp. Replace energy and electrolytes by nibbling food and drinking plenty of water. It'll pay off in greater energy and a feeling of well-being on the trail.

Most Seniors like to hike with others — just pick good companions, ones whose interests are similar to yours. Try, too, finding hiking partners who go at about the same pace as you. It's tiring to either wait on a slower hiker or rush to catch up with someone who blazes down the trail. Fortunate, indeed, is the hiker who can share the trail with an interesting companion — take good care of them; they're valued friends.

Whether you go with others or hike alone, though, follow your own interests. It's your hike, and you should have the time to enjoy it at your own pace and in your own good time. You've earned the right to enjoy your hours on the trail.

A MATTER OF ATTITUDE

Like any other activity, whether or not a day-hike is fun depends on the hiker's attitude and outlook. It won't be hard for you to maintain a positive, up-beat attitude on the trail. It's surprising, though, how many younger hikers fail to develop a positive mental outlook — they see a day-hike as a competitive exercise rather than an enjoyable outing. With age often comes wisdom, and it may be a mark of wisdom to maintain a positive attitude. Most Seniors seem to be good at that, perhaps because we've learned more about ourselves and no longer have to prove our worth.

By far the most important trail technique is to develop a well-honed sense of enjoyment. The southwestern national parks and monuments are places of delight. The Senior, hiking at his own pace and following his own interests, sees before him an unending panorama of natural beauty — clouds changing before his eyes, new and pleasing landscapes opening before him, plants and animals in incredible variety. What better place for a Senior to be?

7

SAFE HIKING
FOR SENIORS

Seniors are justifiably concerned about their physical safety in the backcountry, even though our southwestern national parks and monuments are far safer than most Senior's own homes. The majority of us have spent our lives in urban surroundings, protected from hostile natural environments. We've been able to count on society to protect us from discomfort, providing heat, protection, health care, food, water, shelter, entertainment and all the other needs of civilized life. If it gets dark, light is as close as the nearest electrical outlet. We can banish cold or heat by setting the thermostat higher or lower. Water and food, sanitary facilities, shelter, communication, health care, all the requirments for a safe life are supplied by society — as long as we stay in the city.

When a Senior steps off the blacktop and starts a day-hike into the backcountry, though, conditions are reversed. He becomes a visitor in an unfamiliar environment. Is the environment hostile or benign? Is it dangerous or safe? What does a Senior hiker do if he gets lost, how can he escape the hazards of an uncontrolled landscape? Will he be assured, even, that his car and campsite are safe?

Until you've gained some experience, you'll probably be asking yourself these or similar questions. It's normal — after all, you're entering a new world, and it has to be explored carefully. But a word of encouragement is in order — national parks and monuments are reasonably safe places, and day-hiking can be as safe and comfortable as the hiker wants to make it. Like so many other things, good planning and common sense set the stage for a safe, enjoyable experience.

SAFETY STARTS WITH GOOD PLANNING

Most Seniors are intelligent people who long ago learned the importance of laying good plans. You'll have no trouble planning your day-hikes so they're safe and enjoyable. There are some things you'll always want to keep in mind: weather, routes, trail conditions, your own personal interests, and your own limitations.

WEATHER — BE READY FOR A CHANGE

Weather is one of the most important considerations in planning your day-hike. A change in the weather can put even the most experienced hiker in danger, especially if he becomes complacent. A day that starts sunny and warm can quickly become wet and cold, bringing the danger of hypothermia. Those clouds that pile so majestically on the horizon may bring lightning and drenching rains when they move overhead. The Senior hiker will ignore the possibility of bad weather at his own peril.

You can't plan for every kind of weather, of course, but you can prepare for the most likely and most dangerous weather conditions. If you carry clothing adequate for the season and locality, plus enough extra clothing to keep you warm and dry, you'll usually be in good shape. The most dangerous weather conditions, of course, are those that affect your ability to maintain your body temperature at its normal level. Wet, windy and cool conditions can lead to hypothermia, and hot, dry conditions may result in heat overload. The addition or removal of clothing is the key to survival when weather conditions change. Always, then, carry clothing adequate to respond to the most likely weather conditions and the most likely changes. If you're prepared, you can laugh at any but the harshest weathers, confident that you'll be safe and comfortable.

CHOOSE A ROUTE THAT'S RIGHT FOR YOU

You should pick your routes with some care when planning your day-hike. Not all of us are in good enough physical shape to make it to the top of Rocky Mountain National Park's Longs Peak, so picking the summit of that mountain as a destination for a day-hike isn't really reasonable. If you don't know what your body is capable of, choose moderate trails until you have enough miles behind you to confidently attempt more difficult hikes. The trail descriptions in Part Two can be of help as you choose trails appropriate to your conditioning and interests. As you hike more and more, you'll want to try progressively more challanging trails. At the start, though, plan your route so that you always have reserves of energy and time. You'll not only be safer and more comfortable on the hike, you'll enjoy it far more.

GET INFORMATION ON TRAIL CONDITIONS

Trail conditions also affect your safety on a day-hike. Poor, rough or steep trails take more time and energy than do smooth, well-maintained and more-or-less level trails.

Part Two gives an idea of the trail conditions for several hikes in each southwestern park and monument. Consult that part of the guide when planning your hike.

It's a good idea, too, to visit with the rangers about your hike when you pick up your backcountry permit. Trail conditions change, and the rangers will be able to tell you about the condition of trails in their park or monument, including trails that aren't mentioned in this book.

You'll want to choose trails that fit your interests, the amount of time you have to spend, and your physical condition. Avoid trails that are too difficult for you, or are too long. Fatigue is not only a dangerous physical condition, but a debilitating mental one as well. Safety dictates careful choice of trails and destinations.

PLAN YOUR DAY-HIKES AROUND YOUR PERSONAL INTERESTS

Try to plan your hike around your personal interests, whether they be as definite as wanting to photograph an elk herd, or as vague as simply wanting to get away from the crowd. There are valid reasons for making plans based on your own interests — it gives you a definite goal, and keeps your spirits high. You tend to see more and understand more if you're interested in what you're doing. If you're alert to your surroundings, you're going to be alert to possible hazards as well. Besides, it's your hike, and you deserve to get what you want out of it.

UNDERSTAND YOUR OWN LIMITATIONS

You already have an idea of your own personal limitations, but chances are they're not as limiting as you probably think. As you hike more and more you'll find that not only are you getting better and stronger, but your sense of what's possible will be increasing as well. That's as it should be. Remember, though, that some things are reasonable and some aren't. Don't get carried away and become careless as you become more experienced. Often it isn't the novice who gets into trouble — it's the old hand who forgets or ignores his own limitations.

DECIDING WHEN TO TURN BACK

No matter how well you've planned your day-hike, the time will come when you'll have to decide whether to continue your hike or turn back. Experienced mountaineers have learned to retreat in the face of bad weather, approaching darkness or incipient fatigue. It's hardly a mark of wisdom to continue a hike when you don't feel up to going further.

Certainly you should turn back if the weather deteriorates beyond what you feel you can comfortably handle. You should also shorten your hike if you feel ill or fatigued. There's little to be gained from going on if you aren't enjoying yourself. If there's a still, small voice telling you it's time to head back to the trailhead, pay attention. It may be the voice of discretion.

Only you can decide when you've had enough. Just remember that false pride and overconfidence can let you to get in over your head. When you think it's prudent to head home, do so. You can always complete your hike another day.

IF YOUR PLANS ARE UNUSUAL

If your plans involve anything unusual — hiking off the trails, following unusual routes or hiking at unusual times of day or season, be sure to indicate those things when you talk to rangers about your hike, and make sure the rangers understand your plans. Mention your route, when you'll start and return from your hike, where your car will be parked, the kinds and amount of gear you'll have with you, the amount of experience you've had on similar excursions, and anything appropriate about your health. Be sure to discuss your plans with the rangers — their knowledge of their park is valuable, and they can tell you if you've made adequate plans for what you want to do. In addition, talking over your plans with the rangers will alert them to the fact that you're trying something different. They'll keep an eye on your car and if you don't return, they can begin search efforts that much sooner.

Backcountry permits for day-hikes are not required in most national parks and monuments. However, rangers are so concerned about your safety that they encourage you to inform them of your plans if you're the least bit concerned about the hike. This is especially important if your hike is an unusual one or is off the marked trails. The information, among other things, tells the Park Service personnel where and when to start looking for you if you're overdue. Should you be in one of the very few parks that do require a backcountry permit for day-hiking, you'll be required to check your plans with the rangers anyway.

It's always prudent to leave word with a responsible (and I mean really responsible) person. Give him or her all the information a backcountry permit would require, and indicate in writing both your physical condition and a definite time for your return. Of course, it's imperative that you inform the Park Service or your friend of your safe return. It's very embarrassing to be the object of an unnecessary search and rescue mission.

WHAT TO DO IF YOU BECOME SEPARATED, LOST, ILL OR INJURED

Your chances of becoming separated, lost, ill or injured on a day-hike are very slight, frightening as that experience might be. If you or a companion should become ill, injured or lost, there are some things you can do to remedy the situation.

First, stay calm, difficult as that may sound. Remember the acronym, **S-T-O-P** — *Sit, Think, Observe and Plan*. Sitting helps overcome panic, letting you make decisions based on rational thinking rather than fears and emotions. Think about your difficulty and how to resolve it, but don't imagine the outcome as being disastrous. Observe the predicament you're in and assess your resources (the things in your pack, your emergency and first-aid gear, you own knowledge and so on). Then plan your immediate actions. The acronym *STOP* is a word to remember — it can save you much worry and anxiety if you get into difficulty.

If there's a health emergency on the trail, of course you'll want to take quick action. Each case will be different, and you'll have to use your best judgement about how to react. The decision of whether to leave the victim and go for help or whether to wait until other hikers come along is a heavy one. The answer will depend on your own assessment of the situation — circumstances will dictate what you do after you've taken care of the most obvious life-threatening problems. Again, **S-T-O-P** (Sit, Think, Observe and Plan) is the word to remember. If you do that, there's little doubt that the outcome will be positive.

If you or a companion are lost or separated from your party, then you face another difficult choice. You'll have to decide whether or not to try to get "unlost". If a person is truly lost, it's best in nearly all cases for the lost soul to stay right where he is. Let the rest of the group or other searchers find you. This is especially true at night. Little purpose is served by wandering around blindly. Spend your time, rather, in conserving energy and making yourself comfortable. Remember that whistle in your emergency gear? Give a toot on it once in a while. You won't be lost long.

Accidents do occassionally happen, but usually to those who are unprepared. If you discussed your hike with a ranger, made adequate plans and are carrying the recommended first-aid and emergency gear, you have little to worry about — a comforting thought if something ever should happen on the trail.

AVOIDING HAZARDS

Safe as our national parks and monuments are, it's worthwhile to have a basic knowledge of the symptoms and treatment of conditions that worry a lot of Seniors. Some of these hazards are only irritating, but others can be life-threatening.

AVOIDING THINGS THAT BITE, POKE, STING OR OTHERWISE MAKE YOU FEEL BAD

There are things in the southwestern backcountry that have hurt people, but in general the dangers have been greatly exaggerated. Most of us can avoid trouble with snakes, scorpions, spiders, gila monsters and cacti by using a little extra care. We can sidestep the dangers of heat-related and cold-related injuries by being well-prepared for changeable conditions, and using common sense will help avoid other injuries, illnesses and discomforts.

INJURIES CAUSED BY HEAT AND COLD

The human body is designed to function best at a sub-tropical temperature. Any time the core organs (heart, lungs and brain) are too hot or too cool, the body ceases to function efficiently. Over-heating and over-cooling are dangerous conditions — the Senior hiker should know not only how to avoid them, but how to recognize and treat them as well.

It's important that each group carry an adequate first-aid and emergency kit, and be prepared to use it if needed. The kit should include a supply of rock salt or salt tablets in addition to the items normally found in a good first-aid kit. Most of us have little if any experience with heat-related or cold-related emergencies. Here are some problems, with their solutions:

HYPOTHERMIA

Hypothermia is the greatest health hazard you'll encounter while hiking in the Southwest's national parks and monuments. It's caused by excessive loss of body heat, which results in cooling the core-organs — the heart, lungs and brain. Hypothermia is usually associated with wet, cool, and windy conditions — hence the great emphasis on carrying extra clothing to protect you from the effects of wind and rain.

Hypothermia can be prevented by avoiding wet and windy condtions — if you see a storm coming, put on raingear before you get soaked, and seek shelter out of the wind. It's that simple — if you're prepared for changing weather and alert to its dangers. To avoid hypothermia wear or carry protective clothing, stay dry and out of the wind, maintain your energy level by eating and drinking well both before and during the hike.

Always have some sort of raingear with you, and carry at least a light jacket or sweater even in summer. Should you or a companion become chilled, do whatever is necessary to rewarm the victim. But how do you recognize hypothermia's symptoms, and how do you treat it? Here's some information you'll find helpful:

Symptoms: a. intense shivering; *b.* fatigue or numbness; *c.* stumbling, poor coordination; *d.* slurred speech; *e.* careless or "don't care" attitude

To treat: a. prevent further heat loss; *b.* replace wet clothing and get out of the wind; *c.* give the victim hot drinks; *d.* supply external heat (snuggle up with the victim, warm him by a fire, do anything necessary to provide warmth)

Hypothermia is a dangerous condition — it's much better to avoid it than have to treat a victim. Use common sense, carry enough extra clothing and raingear and be prepared to turn back if the weather changes.

INJURIES CAUSED BY OVERHEATING

There are other injuries that are heat-related; the most common in the Southwest are those that involve overheating and dehydration. To avoid these problems, eat sensibly and drink plenty of fluids. It's important that the body be able to cool itself by sweating, and that the electrolytes in the blood and body-fluids don't become depleted.

Naturally, you want your day-hike to be comfortable, so in hot country plan to hike in the early or late part of the day when you can avoid the most intense heat. Take plenty of water, and unless your physician has recommended that you limit your salt intake, make use of salt tablets or add some additional salt to your food. Here are the three most common heat-related problems:

Heat cramps: caused by loss of electrolytes due to excessive sweating and the loss of too much salt. Prevention includes extra salt with food or water.

> *Symptoms: a.* muscle cramps in legs or abdomen; *b.* pain accompanying the cramps; *c.* profuse sweating

> *To treat: a.* move victim to a cooler place; *b.* give victim salted drinking water (one teaspoon salt to one quart of water); *c.* gently massage the cramped muscles; *d.* get medical help if problem is serious

Heat exhaustion: circulatory problem. Blood is transported from the body's core to the surface of the body, resulting in insufficient return of blood to the heart and brain, leading to collapse.

> *Symptoms: a.* weak pulse; *b.* rapid and unusally shallow breathing; *c.* skin moist or cool, face flushed or pale; *d.* general weakness; *e.* profuse sweating; *f.* dizziness; *g.* unconsciousness

> *To treat: a.* move victim to a cooler place; *b.* keep victim lying down with his feet elevated; *c.* remove as much of victim's clothing as possible; *d.* give cool, salted water; *e.* cool body by convection or conduction, but do not allow to chill; *f.* get medical help if victim does not respond to treatment

Heat stroke: a true emergency, since the heat-controlling centers of the brain are affected. The clue to this condition is that the skin is **HOT** and **DRY**.

> *Symptoms: a.* sudden onset of condition; *b.* hot, flushed, dry skin; *c.* dilated pupils; *d.* pulse is full

and fast; *e.* breathing is fast at first, becoming shallow and faint; *f.* early loss of consciousness; *g.* muscle twitching, leading to convulsions; *h.* body temperature of 105 degrees or more

To treat: a. move victim to a cool place; *b.* cool victim by any means possible; *c.* be prepared to give mouth-to-mouth resuscitation

OTHER IRRITATIONS, LARGE AND SMALL

Very few Senior hikers will ever have to worry about hypothermia, heat overload, or rattlesnakes. Most of us will spend our time concerned with insects, poison ivy or depredations of large animals. Here's how to handle some of these irritants.

AVOIDING CLOSE ENOUNTERS
WITH RATTLESNAKES

Probably the most common worry Seniors have about hiking in the Southwest is that they'll encounter a rattlesnake. The chances of seeing, let alone being bitten, by a rattler are very small, and even if bitten the recovery rate is very high (there are only about 10 deaths from rattlesnake bite annually in the US). Still, a person should avoid being bitten. Here are some hints to reduce the risk of meeting a rattler head-on:

Wear protective clothing, such as boots and long pants, especially when hiking cross-country and after dark.

Keep your eyes open — don't put your hands or feet where your eyes can't see, since about 90% of all snake bites are on the extremities.

Rattlers are usually most active at night, so carry and use a flashlight.

Since rattlers tend to seek protective cover, avoid places where they might be resting.

Go around, not over, large rocks, logs and the like, and don't sit on such things without checking first for snakes.

Be particularly careful in climbing rocky cliffs — don't put your hand on a snake or meet one eye-to-eye.

Remember that rattlers are "cold-blooded", so they'll tend to sun themselves on cold days and to be nocturnal during warmer periods. On cool nights they may warm themselves on sun-heated rocks or roadways; again, carrying and using a flashlight is a good idea.

Remember, rattlers don't always rattle before striking.

SNAKE BITE

Most likely you'll never see a rattlesnake — and the odds of being struck by one are even smaller. In addition, rattlers will often strike without injecting venom. The following information is included so you'll know what to do if you or a companion are bitten:

Symptoms: a. pain at site of bite; b. rapid swelling and discoloration which extends toward the heart; c. weakness and giddiness; d. difficulty in breathing; e. nausea and vomiting; f. low blood pressure, with a thready pulse; g. subnormal

temperature; *h.* numbness and tingling of face,
lips, etc.; *i.* double vision or blindness

To treat: a. don't panic; keep calm; *b.* keep the victim
quiet; *c.* immoblize the bitten part, if possible, and
try to keep it below the level of the heart; *d.* apply
LIGHT constriction between the bitten area and
the heart. Never apply constriction so tightly that
the pulse can't be felt below the the constricting
band, or that you can't pass your small finger
between the band and the victim's flesh; *e.* if ice is
available, put an ice-pack over the fang-marks or
the site of the swelling; most of the time this is
the best treatment for a snake-bite; *f.* transport
the victim by litter, if possible. The less effort on
the part of the victim the greater his chances of
recovery; *g.* keep the victim's spirits high —
there's a 99% recovery rate

There are many other animals that might prove to be
dangerous to the desert traveler, but a Senior shouldn't
curtail his enjoyment of the desert by living in fear of the
organisms found there. By using common sense and exercising caution, a person can feel quite safe in the southwestern national parks and monuments.

INSECTS

Biting or stinging insects can be a nuisance, even on the
desert. Unless you're one of the lucky few who aren't
bothered by insects, you'll want to invest in a good grade of
insect repellent. Since some compounds are themselves
irritating to sensitive skins, you may have to try several
until you find a particular brand that not only deals with
insects, but doesn't bother you, either.

For most insects, as well as ticks and other minute critters, using the insect repellent as directed will control their depredations. If you supplement the repellent with long pants, long-sleeved shirts and other protective clothing, nothing should bother you, not even those tiny black flies that persist in biting any exposed flesh.

A very few Senior hikers are allergic to bee or wasp stings. If you're among that number, consult your physician, who can prescribe a kit containing injectable anti-shock substances. He'll tell you when and how to use it. You might also want to consider choosing seasons or trails that minimize your exposure to biting or stinging insects. For the rest of us, insects may be something we have to tolerate.

POISONOUS PLANTS

Luckily, there are relatively few poisonous plants in the Southwest — but they can make you miserable if you're unfortunate enough to find them. Poison ivy and poison oak are occassional problems, usually in canyon bottoms and on well-vegetated hillsides. They're low-growing plants with bright green leaflets in sets of three. They usually grow in small patches in reasonably moist habitats. The irritant is contained in a heavy oil produced by the plant, an oil that sticks to clothing and can be transferred to the skin by secondary contact. The first contact usually sensitizes the victim, with subsequent contacts giving rise to the rashes that nearly all of us remember from childhood.

It's best, of course, to avoid contact with poison ivy or poison oak, but if you do come in contact with either, try to wash off the oil with strong soap and warm water. If you develop the rash anyway, it can be treated with any of several preparations available at a pharmacy. Some say, too, that an immediate application of household ammonia will stop the itching — worth a try if you can stand the odor.

There are several other troublesome plants you may run across. Nettles are shade-loving inhabitants of moist areas. They produce formic acid, which is injected into the skin through tiny hollow hairs, much like minute hypodermic needles. If you come in contact with a nettle, try covering the affected area with a poultice of mud — it soothes the pain and tends to draw out the nettle's hair as the mud dries.

Cacti, of course, are common in the Southwest. If you're "bitten" by a cactus, carefully try to remove any spines sticking into your skin. Some cactus spines are tipped with an irritating compound, much like a nettle in its effect. If a cactus joint is the culprit, try sliding the teeth of a pocket comb under the joint, then flip it off the skin. Sometimes that works, sometimes it doesn't. You may have to resort to tweezers to remove all the irritating spines.

The best preventive, of course, is to avoid coming into contact with a noxious plant. Second best is to wear clothing that'll help prevent a close acquaintance with poison ivy, cactus or stinging nettles. Treatment for the effects of getting too close come in a distant third.

LARGE ANIMALS

Large animals, unfortunately, are all too rare in the Southwest. You don't have to worry about bears, mountain lions, wolves or other predators. In fact, count yourself lucky if you even see their footprints.

Non-predatory animals are more of a problem, especially if they're cute. You'll be tempted to get close to deer or other photogenic species. Don't. Deer can lash out and inflict a serious wound, and even the cutest chipmunk can give a good nip with its teeth. Animals in the national parks and monuments are wild — parks aren't zoos or petting-farms. Enjoy the wildlife from a distance. They'll be more comfortable, and so will you.

OTHER PREDATORS — YOU AND CRIME IN THE NATIONAL PARKS

Another problem you can avoid is crime. Luckily, muggings and other forms of antisocial behavior are extremely rare in the national parks and monuments. Unfortunately, though, thieves have discovered that careless hikers and campers make good victims. The problem shouldn't disrupt your visit if you take time to make it hard for thieves to strike. Don't, for instance, tempt a thief by leaving valuables in sight. Before you lock your car at the trailhead, put valuable items away and be sure to cover or lock up cameras, binoculars and other tempting items. You'll be safe from thieves if you don't make yourself an easy target. Of course, you'll want to report any suspicious activity, vandalism or theft to a ranger or a campground host.

GENERAL COMMENTS

Most of the things that can hurt a person on the Southwest are things Seniors can avoid by using common sense. For instance, most of us know that if we kick a cactus, some of the spines will probably stick in the toe of our boot — if we poke our hand in the wrong place, it may be bitten by some critter or other. Play it safe; use your head and avoid problems.

Death Valley National Monument   (NPS photo)

Chaco Culture National Historical Park   (NPS photo)

8

ENVIRONMENTAL CONSIDERATIONS FOR SENIOR DAY-HIKERS

Most of the Southwest's national parks and monuments contain wilderness — defined as an area affected primarily by nature, a place where man and his works are substantially lacking. Roads, permanent buildings or other permanent man-made structures are prohibited; even such unnatural activities as insect or disease control and the suppression of wildfires are severely restricted. Natural processes are the dominant forces shaping the landscape — naturally-functioning ecosystems, uncontrolled by man, make wildlands an important and fascinating place to visit and understand.

Seniors who choose day-hiking in the natural settings of the national parks and monuments have a dual responsibility — they must respect and understand the environments and habitats they're enjoying as well as help preserve the highest qualities of the wilderness experience. That means all hikers (not just Seniors) must use the national parks and monuments in such a way that the main goals of wilderness use are served: natural controls and processes must be maintained, and chances for solitude must be enhanced. Practically, meeting these double goals means the national parks and monuments must control the impact visitors make on the environment, and that hikers have to make a few adjustments in what, when, and how they do things.

The wildlands found in the southwestern national parks and monuments are tremendously varied. We're used to thinking of wilderness as encompassing massive peaks, dense forests and mountain valleys — the calender-art conception of wildlands. Southwestern wilderness goes far beyond these usual ideas of natural, wild beauty. The southwestern national parks and monuments include not only mountainous landscapes, but ocean, desert, grassland, and a dozen other kinds of environments. All of them, if they're largely unaffected by the works of man, are true wilderness and worth the time and effort to visit.

Wildlands deserve our care. After all, our nation developed against a background of nearly complete wilderness. Our historic relationship to wilderness shaped our view of ourselves as Americans. How we perceived and used the wilderness frontier made us into a unique people, rather than displaced Europeans.

Few of us don't have pioneers in our family heritage — kinsmen who faced the wild frontier as a fact of life. As Rodrick Nash points out, wilderness shaped us and made Americans a new and unique national group. Now, thanks to the efforts of many thoughtful and dedicated conservationists, we've preserved a few remaining areas representing the wilderness that once covered our continent. Some of the best examples of wildlands and natural areas are in the southwestern national parks and monuments, and are easily accessible to Senior day-hikers.

Today you and I use wilderness as a contrast to an urbanized existence. We visit a national park or monument, sample the wilderness trails there, and come away refreshed and better able to cope with cities, work, neighbors, noise and pollution. Wilderness hikes give us a chance to recharge our batteries.

But the idea of wilderness implies a lack of people, presenting a built-in conflict between the use of wilderness and its very existence, a conflict which gives nightmares to the park managers responsible for preserving wilderness qualities in the face of ever greater numbers of hikers and campers. Everyone, it seems, wants to sample the solitude and isolation available to wilderness hikers — but how can we give everyone solitude and isolation when thousands of hikers want to be on the same trail at the same time? Since wilderness is fragile, and easily lost or damaged, it's essential that each user of the resource contribute to its preservation. As responsible hikers, we have to make sure we're not destroying something we love.

We Seniors have to develop the skill and knowledge to be low-impact hikers. Low-impact hiking demands that we leave the wilderness environment as pristine and unaltered as we found it. It's our responsibility, one that we can't shirk.

Since wilderness is as large as the observer thinks it is, Seniors can easily increase their feeling of seclusion and isloation by avoiding other people. One of the easiest ways a Senior can do this is by visiting a national park or monument during the off-season. An area that can be grossly overcrowded during the winter may be nearly vacant in the spring or fall, making those the best seasons for wilderness hiking. By the same token, hiking a trail in mid-week may mean that you have it all to yourself, although the same trail may be crowded on a weekend. If you want a true wilderness experience, then choose a season or time when most others won't be hiking the same trails.

You can avoid crowds and experience the wilderness best by hiking during periods when park visitation is lowest. For many parks and monuments, this means during the fall, winter and spring months. Mountain parks are busiest during the summer, when more people are free to travel. By arranging your visit for the off-season you'll miss most of the crowd, and winter visits can be delightful. You'll get a glimpse of a winter wilderness most park visitors will never have a chance to see.

Fall, winter and spring, of course, are the most crowded seasons for many desert parks and monuments, but don't let that discourage you. Most desert parks are so large that overcrowding isn't a problem — except in some camp-grounds. Plan to arrive early in the day if you're staying in a campground, or chose a campground away from the centers of activity. With a little planning you can avoid crowded campgrounds and trails — it's worth the effort.

Another thing you can do to increase the solitude and tranquility of wildlands is to avoid making yourself obvious. Leave overly bright clothing and equipment for other times and places. Blaze orange and incandescant pink may be fine for some areas, but definitely not in the back-country of a wilderness area. Noise, too, reduces the feel-ing of solitude, so leave noisemakers, both organic and mechanical, at the trailhead.

One of the main impacts hikers make on natural areas is the destruction of vegetation caused by trampling plants underfoot. For that reason, as well as for safer hiking, it's better to stick to trails than to travel cross-country. Cer-tainly cutting across switchbacks is destructive; those hair-pin turns which trails make as they climb are there for a reason. Loss of vegetation, erosion, and gulley-formation occur quickly on most Southwest soils, so try to stay on trails whenever possible.

In addition, it's worthwhile to wear boots that have soles designed to minimize both compaction of soil and distur-bance of the ground cover, yet which provide good trac-tion. Most well-known brands of boots now use either a ribbed sole or a lug-sole designed to reduce wear-and-tear on vegetation — a small thing, but worth remembering when buying boots. In addition, a little care in choosing your route will help avoid damage to the vegetation.

Water pollution is another problem that's increased by backcountry use. There really isn't any reason for a Senior day-hiker to contribute to the problem. Urination should always be at least a hundred feet from any stream or other water supply, and defecation at least the same distance away. Luckily, nature has provided an excellent sanitary corps in the fungi found a few inches under the soil's surface. If you have to defecate in the field, dig a cat-hole about six to eight inches deep, preserving the ground-cover as best you can. Defecate in the cat-hole and then cover the feces with dirt from the hole. Replace the ground cover, then tamp it down and disguise the site. Toilet paper should be carried out and disposed of properly, since it has a tendency to resurface even if buried completely. The fungus layers in the soil will dispose of the feces fairly quickly, reducing the chance of micro-organisms reaching any water supply or otherwise polluting the environment.

Littering, of course, is out of place anywhere, but espe-cially in the backcountry of a national park or monument. If you've carried anything into the wilderness with you, certainly you can carry it back to the trailhead. Go a step further, though — if you come across litter on your hike, pick it up and take it out with you. It'll help pay for your enjoyment of the area, and clean trails discourage others from littering.

Once in a while a hiker will come on wildlife in the back-country — truly a delightful thing to have happen. It's common courtesy to leave the critters undisturbed — don't approach too closely, and try not to startle them. You're a visitor, but they belong there. Observe them, take your photographs, then move quietly away, happy that you've been fortunate enough to see part of wild nature in action.

Naturally, you should never collect anything in a national park or monument, no matter how tempting it may be. National parks and monuments are preserves — the things found there belong to all of us, not just the first person to pocket an interesting find. Plants, no matter how abundant they seem, should be left undisturbed, and of course animals should be unmolested, too. Natural features, pretty rocks and so on, are protected as well. Many southwestern national parks and monuments contain relics and artifacts of pre-Columbian use of the area. These can tell a story of the lives of former inhabitants, but only if the relics and artifacts are left undisturbed. Follow the advice given on many park bulletin boards — take only photographs, leave only footprints.

Low-impact hiking is an easy skill to learn, and vitally important if we're to leave anything of our country's natural heritage to our children and grandchildren. You can make a contribution to preserving our wildlands by traveling lightly, caring about and understanding the environment you're enjoying.

9

SENIORS AND THE NATIONAL PARK SERVICE

National parks, national monuments, national historic sites, national cultural heritage parks and some national recreation areas are under the jurisdiction of the Department of the Interior's National Park Service. The National Park Service has the mandate to both preserve and protect the lands under their care for the enjoyment of this and future generations. There's a built-in conflict in that mandate — how does one go about providing for present enjoyment without jeopardizing the very things that must be preserved and passed on intact to future generations?

To resolve the conflict between use and preservation, the Park Service has devised sets of regulations which all Seniors should understand. The regulations aren't designed to reduce your enjoyment of a national park or monument, but rather to protect you and the resource the park or monument was set aside to preserve. Since conditions differ from area to area, only the more usual and common policies are outlined here. Remember, policies and regulations may differ from one park to another. It pays to check with a ranger if you have any questions about what you can or can't do — after all, knowing an area's rules and regulations will not only help preserve the park or monument, but will help make your visit safer and more enjoyable.

In addition to protecting the resource and the park visitor, the Park Service has the obligation of interpreting the park or monument to the visitor. Each park or monument provides a number of interpretive services, including publications, nature walks, visitor centers, campfire talks and a host of other programs. By and large, the Park Service does a fine job of helping you learn more about the area you're visiting. By all means take advantage of as many interpretive programs as you can — they'll help you enjoy the park or monument to its fullest.

PERMITS AND OTHER MATTERS

The National Park Service, both as a means of returning money to the national treasury and as a management tool, often requires each park or monument visitor to have one or more kinds of permits in his or her possession. There are entrance fees, camping fees, overnight hiking permits, fire permits, backcountry permits, and at least half a dozen others. Fortunately, Senior day-hikers only have to worry about two or three of these, and the parks and monuments have made it easy for Seniors to get the right permits.

ENTRANCE FEES

All national parks and monuments except the very smallest and most specialized require that visitors pay an entrance fee. The amount varies from park to park, but is usually only a dollar or two for the "purchaser and all who accompany him in a private noncommercial vehicle". Such single-visit permits are usually valid for fourteen days. If you enter the park or monument in anything other than a private vehicle, you'll usually have to pay about fifty cents for a 14-day single-visit permit. Entrance permits are usually valid only for visits to a single park and are usually purchased at the site's entrance station.

If you'll be visiting a series of parks or monuments or making several trips, it may pay to purchase an annual permit. "Golden Eagle" permits currently cost $10, and are one of the great recreational bargains of the decade. Your ten dollars buys you a calander year of entrances to all the National Parks and Monuments.

There's an even greater bargain for Seniors, though. It's the "Golden Age Passport", available without cost to anyone 62 years of age or older. Not only does it give you free entrance to the parks and monuments, it also allows a 50% discount on any camping fees. These permits are available at visitor centers and some entrance stations.

If you or a companion are blind or permanently disabled, you may be entitled to a "Golden Access Pass". Advantages of this pass are the same as those for the Golden Age Passport, but there's no age requirement.

CAMPING FEES

The National Parks and Monuments are required to charge fees for the use of developed, full-service campgrounds. The charge is usually around five dollars per site per night (half that if you have a Golden Age Passport or a Golden Access Pass). There usually isn't a charge if any of the customary services aren't provided, as when water isn't available in the campground. If you're traveling in a motor home or with a travel trailer, remember that few campgrounds in the national parks and monuments have hookups, and that there may be restrictions as to the size of units allowed in a particular campground. You can contact the specific park you'll be visiting for information about facilities for motor homes or travel trailers.

BACKCOUNTRY PERMITS

Backcountry permits are becoming facts of life for hikers in the national parks and monuments. They allow the park service to monitor backcountry and wilderness use, insure that trails don't become overcrowded, and can be important safety factors for the visitor. Permits aren't required for day-hiking on most trails, but may be good things to have for your own safety and peace of mind, especially if you're concerned about your health or physical condition.

Whether required or not, Senior day-hikers can get a free backcountry permit before hitting the trail. In fact, backcountry permits are so important that several parks and monuments (particularly those with fragile archaeological sites or other attractions that need protection) make them mandatory for all hikers regardless of the destination or length of their hike.

You can pick up the free backcountry permit (or its equivalent) at the park or monument's visitor center and usually at other sites as well, including ranger stations. You can usually call ahead to reserve a permit. You should know your route, where you'll leave your car, and the general time of your return. Rangers check parking areas periodically, and will be alterted if you happen to be overdue — but only if you have a backcountry permit. Without the permit, they have no way of knowing whether or not you're on the trail.

When you inquire about a permit, take a moment to visit with the ranger; he or she can give you up-to-date information on trail conditions, weather and other factors that help make your hike safer, more comfortable and more enjoyable. Be sure to get at least a basic map of the area where you'll be hiking, and ask if there are any problems you should anticipate. The rangers are knowledgeable about conditions in the park or monument (thanks in part to Senior hikers like you who report information about unusual things they've encountered on the trails). In addition, the ranger can help you determine if you've picked the right trail for the kind of hike you want to take. He or she can suggest alternative trails that might be less difficult or more enjoyable, or ones that might suit your interests more precisely.

Permits for hiking in the backcountry serve several important functions. They allow the Park Service to monitor backcountry use, insuring that the backcountry doesn't become overcrowded. The permit also notifies the patrol rangers that you're out hiking — they can then begin a search if you're overdue, a most comforting thought should you get into trouble. The ranger's road patrol is also informed of the location of your parked car, and will check on it during their rounds, a pattern that discourages theft and vandalism.

In addition, the permit issued at the visitor center gives an accurate count of the number of people using trails and other facilities that make up visitor services in the southwestern parks and monuments. This information is valuable in allocating resources for parking areas, comfort stations, trail maintenance, ranger and interpretation services and so on. Far from being a nusiance, the free backcountry permit is helpful to both you and the park or monument. Be sure to get one before starting your hike; it's free, it'll add to your margin of safety, and it helps the Park Service manage the lands under their jurisdiction.

PETS

Pets, of course, are not allowed on any trails or in any buildings in the national parks and monuments. Pets are definitely out of place on trails; they're not part of the natural scene, and some pets may disturb or frighten other hikers. In addition, the backcountry of southwestern parks and monuments is foreign to your pet — new sights and smells may make even the best-behaved animal uncomfortable and uncontrollable. Don't risk injuring or frightening your pet by taking him on the trail. He won't enjoy it, and neither will you or other visitors.

Remember, though, that if you leave your pet locked in your car, you should make sure he'll stay comfortable and cool. Sun streaming in through your car's windows can create an unbearable hothouse. If you leave your pet in the car, park in the shade, leave the windows open a bit for ventilation, and leave a dish of water for him. He'll be more comfortable and safer there than on the trail. He'll probably thank you for your thoughtfulness.

COLLECTING OR DISTURBING PARK FEATURES

Collecting plants, animals, geological specimens, pottery sherds or any other relics or objects is, naturally, forbidden. The southwestern parks and monuments were set aside to protect the living organisms, geological, and archaeological features found there. Collecting or disturbing these things means other visitors are deprived from enjoying them. It might appear that a park or monument has an inexhaustible supply of potsherds, attractive stones, intriguing plants and interesting animals, but like all things found in our national parks and monuments, they represent part of our national heritage. Leave then where they are, so other hikers may enjoy their mystery and beauty in a natural, undisturbed setting.

PROTECTING THE PARKS AND MONUMENTS

Another Park Service policy protecting the area's resources is to limit the use of open fires. No open fires are allowed anywhere in some parks and monuments (with the exception of campgrounds and picnic areas). Even when fire danger is low, it's a good idea not to build an open fire. If you want to boil or cook something in the backcounry, carry and use one of the tiny gas stoves designed for backpacking, rather than build an unsightly fire-ring and burn wood which should be left to decay and return its nutrients to the soil.

Yet another way in which you can help preserve our southwestern backcountry is to use trails rather than travel cross-country. Especially damaging is the practice of cutting switchbacks to descend into a canyon. Southwestern cliffsides are usually easily eroded, so use the trail as you ascend or descend. Taking a short cut can also be hazardous, especially if you try to descend a cliff face in a spot where you can't see the route ahead of you. More than one red-faced hiker has had to be rescued when he got himself in a place where he could climb neither up nor down.

As you hike the southwestern parks and monuments, remember to help preserve the area in its natural condition. The less impact you make on the landscape the better. Littering, of course, is never proper. It's just as bad, and probably more damaging, to thoughtlessly tear off a tree's branch to use as a walking stick. The best idea is to leave only your tracks, and take away only your memories of a beautiful day on some backcountry trail in a pristine southwestern park or monument.

VISITOR SERVICES AND THE SENIOR DAY-HIKER

If you should have an emergency in a southwestern park or monument, any Park Service employee can help you. In case of emergency, rangers can always be contacted by phone. In addition, a recorded message giving information about the park or monument and its roads, trails and programs is often available by calling the park or monument. Phones are usually located at entrance stations, campgrounds, ranger stations, stores or other places easily found by visitors. Emergency messages are also usually handled at the visitor centers, entrance stations and campgrounds.

In case of an emergency, contact any park or monument employee, giving the information he'll request. He'll want to know about the location of the emergency, its nature, the condition of the victim, whether or not anyone's with the victim and so on. This information will be important in the Park Service's response to the problem. Be sure you remain available to talk to a ranger if more information is needed.

The southwestern parks and monuments are interesting places, and the more you know about them the more interesting they become. A wide variety of interpretive programs are available for your information and enjoyment while you're visiting a park or monument. In general, the programs are offered during the periods of greatest visitation — Labor Day through Memorial Day for most areas, or throughout the winter for parks or monuments with a lot of winter visitors. Programs, demonstrations, ranger-lead walks, slide-shows and other interpretive activities are listed on schedules posted throughout the park or monument. A reduced schedule of interpretive programs is followed throughout the rest of the year, but a ranger is always available for you to visit with in the visitor centers, which are usually open from about 8-7 during the periods of greatest visitation and from about 8-4:30 during other times.

A FINAL SAFETY REMINDER

Southwestern parks and monuments are delightful places — especially if you take your time to hike and see them at your own pace. Southwestern parks and monuments have elevations ranging from about 230 feet below sea level to well over 14,000 feet — making it necessary to relax and slow down until your body becomes acclimated to the elevation. Most seniors won't even notice the altitude, but if you have heart, circulatory or respiratory problems, take it easy until you feel comfortable and at home with the elevation. Start with short, easy hikes, drink plenty of fluids, and get plenty of rest. Soon you won't even notice the elevation.

It's always a good idea to carry plenty of water while on the trail. During the warmer months take at least two quarts per day for each person (some areas recommend doubling that amount), and take a quart or more with you when hiking during cooler periods. The air tends to be dry, and you may not notice that you're becoming dehydrated until your body sends you some unmistakeable signals. Don't wait that long — carry enough water to slake your thirst frequently. Even in winter, dry air and the physical exercise of hiking can lead to minor dehydration. Carry plenty of water and sip at it often.

You should carry your own water rather than count on water in streams for drinking. Unfortunately, nearly all streams in the Southwest are unsafe as sources for drinking-water. The tiny organism, *Giardia*, is present in all too many streams, and causes a most unpleasant and

persistant intestinal disorder. Carry your own water —
don't count on purifying "natural" water, no matter how
inviting it looks. The risk of intestinal discomfort is too
great to leave to chance.

Other potential dangers, but ones easily avoided, are dis-
eases carried by fleas living on small mammals, mainly
chipmunks, ground squirrels and rabbits. Fleas from these
animals may carry plague organisms, and may transfer the
plague bacteria to pets or human hosts. Avoid contact,
then, with small wild animals — don't feed them, and be
sure to report any sick, sluggish or dead rodents, ground
squirrels, chipmunks, or rabbits to a ranger. Pets may pick
up infected fleas, another good reason to leave pets at
home or in your car when hiking in southwestern parks
and monuments. Your chances of contracting plague are
very, very slight — certainly not great enough to keep you
from enjoying hiking in the Southwest.

There are some noxious and irritating plants and animals
in southwestern parks and monuments, of course, just as
there are elsewhere. Biting insects are rarely a problem,
but can be annoying at times. Again, remember that poison ivy is found along a few of the streams, but usually can
be avoided by staying on the trail. Poisonous plants are
uncommon in southwestern parks and monuments, but to
be on the safe side don't eat any green plants, berries, or
mushrooms unless you're absolutely sure of their
identification.

Poisonous snakes and scorpions, luckily, are not all that
common in southwestern parks and monuments, but to be
on the safe side you should be careful of where you sit or
put your hands. Again, common-sense precautions will
help make your visit safe and enjoyable.

Remember, too, that all the animals you see in the national
parks and monuments are wild. As mentioned before, deer

may allow you to approach closely, but don't do it. They've been known to slash out and inflict painful injuries with their sharp hooves. Other large mammals are fairly rare and seldom seen. If you do spot an elk, mountain lion, bear or other unusual resident of the backcountry, mention your sighting to a ranger; they in turn can tell other visitors, who'll enjoy sharing your excitement.

Of course, it's not good to feed wild animals; your nutritional requirements are probably not the same as theirs, and feeding them encourages wild animals to overpopulate some areas, leading to hunger and starvation when the source of food goes home.

With a little planning and care, your day-hikes in the Southwest's national parks and monuments will be safe, enjoyable and rewarding. The following pages will give you an idea of what's waiting on the trail. I hope you'll enjoy hiking them as much as I have.

Sequoia National Park   (NPS photo)

PART II —
THE DAY-HIKES

Now that you're ready to go hiking in the southwestern national parks and monuments, you'll need to pick trails that suit your particular interests, schedules, and physical abilities. There are hundreds of fine hikes, ranging from short and pleasant strolls to longer and more difficult treks. I've chosen thirty-one hikes to include here; all are suitable for Seniors. Each trail I've hiked has been delightful — I've enjoyed myself, been comfortable, and felt safe while hiking. Pick one or more of these trails, follow the hints I've given, and I think you'll enjoy them as much as I have.

Whether you're an expert hiker or a novice, you'll need some information about where you're going, how to get there, what to expect, what to take, and who to contact for more information. You, too, can make your hikes safe, enjoyable, and comfortable.

I've arranged information so that a touring Senior can easily and quickly find details about the areas he's visiting. In addition, the information about each specific park or monument is presented so that important points are outlined for quick reference.

First, of course, is general information about the park or monument:

GETTING THERE gives you the best and most direct route to the park or monument

ABOUT DAY-HIKING outlines the information you'll need for permits, who to contact for up-to-date information, and other important matters

PARK INFORMATION indicates who to contact in the park for both general and specific information about the area, its roads and trails, interpretive activities, and so on

CAMPGROUNDS gives you the name and location of the area's developed camping facilities

REPORT EMERGENCIES to the ranger stations indicated, either by phone or in person

NEAREST PHYSICIAN indicates the closest medical facilities; remember, too, that most Park Service personnel are trained in emergency medical treatment

PARK ADDRESS gives the mailing address you should use when writing the park or monument for information

WEATHER outlines the general weather patterns of the area — this can be quite useful in planning your visit and hikes

Secondly, one or two trails for each of the twenty-one southwestern national parks and monuments is discussed. The following information is given for each of the thirty trails outlined in Part II:

DISTANCE is given either one-way or round-trip, depending on the usual or most convenient route

TRAILHEAD indicates the starting point for the day-hike; the exact location is easily found on the free park brochure available at entrance stations and visitor centers; in addition, each trailhead is associated with a parking area where you may leave your vehicle

ELEVATION of the start of the hike, as well as the highest point along the trail, is given

GRADES are subjective things, but I've indicated a conservative estimate of the grade (and hence the difficulty) of each trail

RANGER STATION indicates the location of the nearest ranger station to the trailhead

BEST SEASONS gives my judgement of the finest times of year to be on a particular trail

PLANT COMMUNITIES you're likely to notice along the trail are indicated in the terminology used by park interpretors in each park or monument

COMMON PLANTS include the most noticable or most common varieties (you'll undoubtedly see dozens of other plants in addition to those I've listed)

COMMON ANIMALS listed for each trail are only those which are most common; remember, most animals are shy — don't expect to see them all on a short visit to an area

NOTES are included concerning unusual hazards, safety, and comfort concerns; read the notes carefully — they contain some valuable hints which will help make your day-hike more safer and more enjoyable

The third and final section outlines the day-hike itself. Use this section as a starting point in planning your hike. Since part of the thrill of being on the trail is in discovering pleasures for oneself, I have avoided giving a detailed itinerary — I think you'll find the trail descriptions complete enough to increase your comfort and enjoyment of the hike, while still leaving you free to travel on your own. Remember, though, that conditions change — it's your responsibility to make sure you're properly informed and prepared for any hike you undertake (another good reason to check with the rangers before you hit the trail).

Channel Islands National Park   (NPS photo)

1

CHANNEL ISLANDS NATIONAL PARK

Channel Islands National Park includes five of the eight main islands lying in California's Santa Barbara Channel. Because of their unusual natural and cultural resources the islands and surrounding waters were declared a National Marine Sanctuary in 1980. Today Senior hikers can visit Anacapa and Santa Barbara Islands to sample their unique environment, and thanks to the cooperation of island landowners, can request permits to visit the other three islands included in the national park. Birdwatchers will especially enjoy Santa Barbara and Anacapa Islands — brown pelicans, barn and burrowing owls and a multitude of sea birds make their homes on the islands. If you're planning a visit to the park, be sure to contact the Visitor Center (located on the mainland) for hiking information, and see the park's concessionaire to arrange for transportation to the islands. I think you'll enjoy hiking in such unusual surroundings — especially if you start with the East Anacapa Island Nature Trail. It gives a good overview of this unusual national park.

GETTING THERE: Visitors northbound on US 101 should take the Victoria Avenue Exit at Ventura, CA; southbound visitors should use the Seaward Avenue Exit

ABOUT DAY-HIKING: Special regulations apply; contact park headquarters (805-644-8262); transportation to the islands is by private boat or on the park concessionaire's vessels

PARK INFORMATION: Visitor Center (644-8262)

CAMPGROUNDS: Anacapa and Santa Barbara Islands only; required permits are available at park headquarters; no national park campgrounds on the mainland, but there are many state parks nearby

REPORT EMERGENCIES: Visitor Center (644-8262) or use VHF Marine Band 16 (patrol vessels "Sea Ranger" and "Pacific Ranger"); ranger stations on Anacapa Island, Santa Barbara Island, San Miguel Island

NEAREST PHYSICIAN: Ventura, California

PARK ADDRESS: Channel Islands National Park, 1901 Spinnaker Drive, Ventura, California 93001

WEATHER: Temperate, with daytime highs in the 80s and nightly lows in the 50s. Nighttime and morning fogs are common; frost very rare. Most rains fall during the winter months. Exposed areas are likely to be windy throughout the year.

EAST ANACAPA ISLAND NATURE TRAIL

DISTANCE: 1.5 miles round-trip

TRAILHEAD: Anacapa Island Visitor Center

ELEVATION: Start 100 feet; highest 250 feet

GRADES: Easy to moderate

RANGER STATION: Anacapa Island Visitor Center

BEST SEASONS: Year-round

PLANT COMMUNITIES: Coastal bluff (sea cliff, Coreopsis, and iceplant communities); coastal sage scrub, island grassland, island oak communities

COMMON PLANTS: Iceplant, figwort, kelp, giant coreopsis (tree sunflower), prickly pear cactus, cholla, California sage

COMMON ANIMALS: Western gull, California sea lion, gray whale, alligator lizard, brown pelican, deer mouse

NOTE: Carry an ample supply of water; trail approaches cliffs which may be undercut and weak — stay on the trail; no shade on island; making a landing on the island requires using a small skiff, climbing a ladder and then negotiating a steep series of stairs

The **EAST ANACAPA ISLAND NATURE TRAIL** is the most easily accessible day-hike in the national park, and well worth the effort and expense it takes to get there. The trail starts at the small visitor center on East Anacapa Island; making it to the visitor center is an adventure in itself, involving taking a boat from the mainland, transferring to a small skiff to reach the ladder by which visitors land, and then climbing a series of steps (154 of them, to be exact), then taking the short trail which leads to the island's visitor center. The first thing most visitors notice is the foghorn and lighthouse — don't approach these too closely, since the foghorn is loud enough to damage your hearing.

As you hike along the trail, take a look at the broken foundations of old buildings, now covered by iceplant, an exotic species which tends to replace several of the native plants in areas where it can thrive. A short distance further is a building containing two large water tanks. It was designed to look like a church on the theory that people are less likely to take potshots at a church than at the redwood water tanks inside (an example of protective camouflage in architecture). Just past the "church" is Cathedral Cove, a delightful place to stop and look for California sea lions playing among the kelp, as well as for observing western gulls, brown pelicans and cormorants. If you're there in January or February watch for the spouts of migrating gray whales. This is one of the best places to spot them.

A short distance down the trail is an area covered with tree sunflowers or giant coreopsis. For most of the year this plant appears lifeless — in late winter and early spring, though, the flowers appear, transforming the island into a striking golden paradise. The trail passes the campground and picnic area before continuing to the west end of the island. As you hike along, notice the cacti, both prickly pear and cholla, as well as morning glories and gumplants. Near the western headland hikers can sometimes see several other islands — also part of the national park. The trail takes you past a large gull rookery (in use from about April through July) and back to the campground. There you can take the right fork to get a good view of the lighthouse and the remainder of the island, and to return to the landing cove for your voyage back to the mainland.

I think you'll enjoy hiking on this island — plan to visit the others in this remarkable park. Each island is different, but all offer the Senior hiker an unusual experience.

2

PINNACLES NATIONAL MONUMENT

Pinnacles National Monument centers around the jagged, weathered remnants of an ancient volcano; the pinnacles thrust into the sky, offering a rugged contrast to the low, rolling landscape around them. Much of the park's vegetation is Coast Chaparral, one of only two complete examples of this interesting vegetative association in the national park system. The pinnacles themselves are the northern remnants of a volcano which happened to lie astride the San Andreas Fault. The volcano split as two tectonic plates — pieces of the earth's crust — slid under each other. Part of it remained on the stationary plate while the other part slid some 195 miles north to form the present Pinnacles National Monument. It didn't happen all at once, of course, but took place over millions of years. In fact, the plate on which the pinnacles rest is still moving at the rate of about an inch and a half a year. You'll like hiking in this world of unusual geology and intriguing landscapes; try the Old Pinnacles Trail — it's a good introduction to this intimate park.

GETTING THERE: The park, which is 34 miles south of Hollister and 5 miles off CA 25, is often approached from the south via King City. The west-side entrance from US 101 at Soledad isn't connected by road with the east side of the park, so plan your route with some care.

ABOUT DAY-HIKING: Permits are not mandatory, but Seniors may check in with rangers at the Visitor Center on the east side (404-389-4578) or at Chaparral Ranger Station (389-4526) on the west side if concerned about trails or trail conditions

MONUMENT INFORMATION: Visitor Center (389-4578) or Chaparral Ranger Station (389-4526)

CAMPGROUNDS: Chaparral Campground (west side of monument); Pinnacles Campground (privatly owned, east side of monument)

REPORT EMERGENCIES: Visitor Center (389-4578), Chaparral Ranger Station (389-4526), entrance station or to any ranger or employee

NEAREST PHYSICIAN: Hollister, California; Soledad, California

MONUMENT ADDRESS: Pinnacles National Monument, Paicines, California 95043

WEATHER: Summers and fall are hot and dry. Rainfall averages about 16 inches per year, falling mostly in winter and early spring. Winters are mild, with nightly lows seldom much below freezing.

OLD PINNACLES TRAIL

DISTANCE: 3.4 miles one-way

TRAILHEAD: Entrance to Chalone Creek Picnic Area

ELEVATION: Start 1000 feet; highest 1401 feet

GRADES: Easy, with one steep, narrow section

RANGER STATION: Visitor Center or Chaparral Ranger Station

BEST SEASONS: Spring, summer, fall

PLANT COMMUNITIES: broadleaf (mesic) chaparral on north-facing hillsides; oak-grass savanna on south-facing hillsides

COMMON PLANTS: Digger pine, blue oak, coast live oak, greasewood, toyon, manzanita, arroyo willow, mountain mahogany, California juniper

COMMON ANIMALS: Blacktailed jackrabbit, brush rabbit, Merriam's chipmunk, western gray squirrel, coyote, wild Russian boar, scrub jay, plain titmouse, turkey vulture, mourning dove

NOTE: Water in creek is questionable in quality — carry an ample supply of clean water; low ceilings and unsure footing in cave area; a flashlight is required for the route through Balconies Cave (if you forget your flashlight you can follow the trail along the cliffs above the cave)

The **OLD PINNACLES TRAIL** begins at the Chalone Creek Picnic Area, wanders through an old campground (now being reclaimed), then follows an abandoned road along Chalone Creek. As you hike this pleasant route notice the dense riparian or stream-side vegetation along the creek bottom, the thick chaparral on cool and moist north-facing slopes, and the lovely open oak-and-grassland savanna on the hotter, drier north-facing hillsides. The creek bottom is cool, shady and usually has a good breeze blowing through the blue oaks, manzanita, toyon, greasewood, and digger pines. Notice, too, the occasional breccia boulders beside the wide trail.

After following the creek for about 2.3 miles the trail divides, with the right fork going up and along the cliffside. The main trail enters Balconies Cave, formed by rockslides filling the canyon bottom. You'll need a flashlight to follow the trail through the cave, and must be able to do some bending and stooping to avoid bumping your head on the few areas with a low ceiling. Although the trail through the cave can be slippery when wet, by all means follow the path into the cave — it's much cooler and more refreshing than the trail on the cliffs above. At the west portal to the cave you emerge into a pleasant area of oaks and grasses; enjoy a few moments here before hiking another mile to Chaparral Campground.

You can return to the Chalone Creek Picnic Area by retracing your route on the Old Pinnacles Trail, or by hiking one of the upper trails back to the Visitor Center and then taking the Bear Gulch Trail to the Chalone Creek Picnic Area. I think you'll enjoy the Old Pinnacles Trail — it's like taking a stroll down a quiet country road.

3

SEQUOIA-KINGS CANYON NATIONAL PARKS

Sequoia-Kings Canyon National Parks (two national parks administered as a single unit) offer the Senior some of the best mountain hiking to be had anywhere in the world. Hundreds of miles of trails lead into a wilderness backcountry dominated by glacially carved valleys, shining granite domes and peaceful alpine valleys under the crest of the Sierra Nevada. And, of course, Seniors can hike among peaceful groves of giant sequoias, absorbing the majesty and patience of these stately survivors from antiquity. Because of the distances involved, most Seniors will find that their hiking (at least on their first visit to the park) will be centered around areas that are easily reached from the highways. You should plan your hiking to take advantage of the coolness of the mountain summers; remember that several of the highways are closed by snowfall from late fall through early spring. Hike the trails outlined below — you'll agree that Sequoia-Kings Canyon is a special place.

GETTING THERE: The park can be approached either from Visalia, CA, via CA 198 or from Fresno on CA 180

ABOUT DAY-HIKING: Permits aren't mandatory, but it's suggested that you notify rangers of any unusual plans, routes or problems

PARK INFORMATION: Ash Mountain Visitor Center (209-565-3456; 565-3351 for recorded informational message); the official National Park Service phone number is 209-565-3341

CAMPGROUNDS: Lodgepole, Dorst in Giant Forest Area; Atwell Mill and Cold Springs in Mineral King area; Potwisha, Buckeye Flat and South Fork at lower elevations; Sunset, Azelea and Crystal Springs in the Grant Grove area; Sheep Creek, Sentinel, Canyon View and Moraine in the Cedar Grove area

REPORT EMERGENCIES: Any visitor center, ranger station, ranger or employee, or by calling 565-3341 (or 911 for emergencies only)

NEAREST PHYSICIAN: Three Rivers, California; Visalia, California; Fresno, California

PARK ADDRESS: Sequoia-Kings Canyon National Parks, Three Rivers, California 93271

WEATHER: Lower elevations: mild, wet winters and hot, dry summers; annual precipitation averages 26 inches, but summer rains are rare. Middle elevations: warm days and cool evenings during the summer; 40-45 inches average annual precipitation, most occuring in winter, but summer afternoon thunderstorms are not unusual. Higher elevations: mild for high mountains, but nightly summer lows may drop to freezing or below; be prepared for a rare afternoon thundershower.

BARTON'S POST CAMP-HART TREE
FALLEN GOLIATH LOOP TRAIL

DISTANCE: 6.0 miles round-trip

TRAILHEAD: Redwood Canyon Trailhead (five miles south of Grant Grove Visitor Center, then right on dirt road at Quail Flat for 1.5 miles, then left into parking area)

ELEVATION: Start 6600 feet; highest 6800 feet

GRADES: Moderate, with several easy sections

RANGER STATION: Grant Grove Visitor Center

BEST SEASONS: Spring, summer, fall (or winter for cross-country skiing)

PLANT COMMUNITIES: Sequoia-mixed conifer forest; riparian or stream-side

COMMON PLANTS: Giant sequoia, white fir, sugar pine, incense cedar, dogwood, cinquefoil, leopard lily, monkey flower, red columbine, ferns

COMMON ANIMALS: Mule deer, black bear, chipmunk, ground squirrel, Douglas squirrel, mountain chickadee, red-breasted nuthatch, black phoebe

NOTE: Surface water may be contaminated — carry good water with you; the road to the trailhead is steep, narrow and dusty, but safe if driven at slow speed

The BARTON'S POST CAMP-HART TREE-FALLEN GOLIATH LOOP TRAIL begins on an old jeep road leading away from the Redwood Canyon parking area; the trail immediately drops into the valley of Barton Creek, passing impressive specimens of giant sequoias, incense cedars and sugar pines. The trail in this area is lined with cinquefoils, lupines and dogwood, and the air is filled with birds' songs. The feeling one has on this seldom-used trail is of peace and tranquility — truly a remarkable experience.

At the trail junction a short distance from the parking area, take the left fork for Tunnel Log and Hart Tree. You'll see abundant evidence of wild-fires in this spot, including sequoias with charred "cat-faces", some of which have produced a reddish sap. Notice as well the abundance of young sequoias in the burned-over areas; fire is a natural part of the sequoia's environment, and is necessary for the forest's regeneration. The trail continues to descend, crossing Barton Creek at the site of an old logging camp. The small moist areas along the stream support a profusion of flowers, including monkey flowers, leopard lilies, horsetail rush and ferns. There are many large trees in this area, including incense cedars and sugar pines which would be considered gigantic anywhere else but are dwarfed by the magnificent sequoias growing beside them.

The trail soon passes a log cabin fashioned from the fallen trunk of a sequoia, then climbs a short slope with much drier conditions; notice that the vegetation changes on the warmer, drier side of the valley, with manzanita and ponderosa pines dominating the more arid hillside. In another mile the trail passes Hart Meadow, a lovely spot with red columbines, corn lily or false hellebore, monkey flowers, leopard lilies and a cool, trickling stream flowing through a classical coniferous forest. In the next half mile the trail passes through yet another sequoia grove; in one place the trail goes through the length of a downed giant — the Tunnel Log. In a short distance you'll pass three fallen sequoias before crossing a small stream with a waterfall;

you can climb on the logs and measure these impressive trees for yourself.

The trail then leads to Hart Tree, one of the largest living sequoias. Take the short spur trail and walk around the base of this giant. In another mile the trail comes to Fallen Goliath, a large and impressive downed sequoia, then goes on to join another old road. Go right on this trail, which follows the creek and detours around a newly fallen sequoia before returning you to the parking area. You'll find this loop trail a peaceful and beautiful hike; spend enough time to enjoy it to the fullest.

RIVER TRAIL-ZUMWALT MEADOW TRAIL

DISTANCE: 2.7 miles one-way

TRAILHEAD: Roaring River Falls parking area, two miles east of Cedar Grove Ranger Station

ELEVATION: Start 4800 feet; highest 5035 feet

GRADES: Easy, with one moderate section

RANGER STATION: Cedar Grove Ranger Station

BEST SEASONS: Spring, summer, fall

PLANT COMMUNITIES: Mixed conifer forest; riparian or stream-side

COMMON PLANTS: Incense cedar, sugar pine, ponderosa pine, white fir, white alder, cottonwood, willows, sierra gooseberry, currant

COMMON ANIMALS: Red-winged blackbird, canyon wren, warblers, mule deer, California gray squirrel

NOTE: Surface water may be unsafe — carry good water with you; the current in the river is deceptively strong — don't attempt to cross or swim the river

The **RIVER TRAIL** begins at the Roaring River Falls parking area, where a short trail leads to good views of a large waterfall. After looking at the falls, take the trail leading to Zumwalt Meadow and Road's End. This trail starts in a hot dry area with manzanita, sage, oaks, ponderosa pines and incense cedars, then follows the river upstream through a beautiful mixed conifer forest. There are open areas with good views of the glacially-carved, Yosemite-like cliffs of the valley, especially where the trail goes up and over moraines left by glaciers which emerged from the side-canyons into the main valley.

In 1.6 miles the trail intersects a short path from the Zumwalt Meadow parking area. Stay on the main trail as it approaches Zumwalt Meadow, then follow the short path around the meadow — it rejoins the main trail to Road's End. Zumwalt Meadow offers fine birdwatching in the spring and early summer; the trail along the meadow's edge goes through a beautiful riparian forest, with more incense cedars, cottonwood, and a profusion of flowers.

After rejoining the main trail, follow it upstream again until you come to another bridge. Cross the river and come out at the Road's End parking area. You can return to your vehicle either by following the River Trail back downstream or by hiking beside the road. You'll be surprised by the different views as you take the River Trail back to your car. I like this trail — it's a great introduction to the Sierra; I think you'll like it, too.

4

JOSHUA TREE NATIONAL MONUMENT

Joshua Tree National Monument is not only a hiker's heaven, it's a novice ecologist's idea of Mecca. Two great deserts meet within the boundaries of the monument, allowing the Senior hiker to sample and compare both landscapes — and both are interesting. If you hike below about 3000 feet elevation, you'll be in the Colorado Desert with its vast creosote bush flats. Above that the slightly cooler and more moist Mojave Desert holds dominion, impressing the Senior hiker with its stands of Joshua trees. As if that weren't enough, a third environment is important here — the oases. Oases with fan palms and cottonwoods indicate those few places where water is near the surface. Drawn to the more moist fan palm oases, birds and other animals are abundant around these islands in the desert. Several short day-hikes can include stops at one or more cool, shady oases. Other short hikes can take you through surrealistic stands of Joshua trees and the free-form sculpture of massive granite outcrops. As part of your visit, plan to hike one or more of the nature-trails at Hidden Valley, Barker Dam, Indian Cove or High View. Joshua Tree National Monument may have the ultimate desert landscape — oases, arroyos, playas, bajadas, desert varnish, pediments, unusual plants and animals — it's here for the Senior hiker to sample and enjoy.

GETTING THERE: Joshua Tree National Monument is 140 miles east of Los Angeles; if coming from the west take I-10 and CA 62 to the towns of Joshua Tree and Twentynine Palms (north entrances). The south entrance is 25 miles east of Indio and can be approached from either east or west, again via I-10.

ABOUT DAY-HIKING: No permit is necessary, but Senior hikers are encouraged to leave an itinerary if considering a more difficult or lengthy day-hike

PARK INFORMATION: Oasis Visitor Center (619-367-7511) or at ranger stations

CAMPGROUNDS: Belle, White Tank, Jumbo Rocks, Ryan, Hidden Valley, Indian Cove, Cottonwood, Black Rock Canyon (the last two have water available, and a camping fee is charged for overnight stays there)

REPORT EMERGENCIES: San Bernardino Interagency Dispatch Office (714-383-5651), Oasis Visitor Center (367-7511), ranger stations, any ranger, or call 911 after business hours (for emergencies only)

NEAREST PHYSICIAN: High Desert Medical Center, Joshua Tree, California

MONUMENT ADDRESS: Joshua Tree National Monument, 74485 National Monument Drive, Twentynine Palms, California 92277

WEATHER: Higher elevations are moderate year-round, but summer temperatures will average in 90s and 100s at lower elevations. Winter lows are in the 30s and 40s with winter highs generally in the 60s. Humidity and precipitation, of course, are quite low.

SKULL ROCK TRAIL

DISTANCE: 1.7 miles round-trip

TRAILHEAD: Loop E of Jumbo Rocks Campground

ELEVATION: Start 4400 feet; highest 4450 feet

GRADES: Very easy

RANGER STATION: Oasis Visitor Center

BEST SEASONS: Fall, winter or spring

PLANT COMMUNITIES: Joshua tree; pinon-juniper woodland

COMMON PLANTS: Joshua tree, creosote bush, prickly pear, cotton-thorn, Mojave yucca, mormon tea, pencil cholla, cat-claw acacia, California juniper, jojoba, pinon pine, turbinella oak, paper-bag bush

COMMON ANIMALS: Desert cottontail, raven, black-tailed jackrabbit, whiptailed lizard, coyote, wood rat

NOTE: There's no water along the trail — carry a filled canteen; intense summer heat may be a problem (hike early or late during the hotter months); rock formations off the trail are deceptively steep — make sure you can climb down whatever you climb up

The **SKULL ROCK TRAIL** goes through some fine examples of Joshua Tree National Monument's striking vegetation and unusual rock formations. It starts in a Joshua tree forest, then leads through an open desert garden filled with Mojave yucca, paper-bag bushes, cotton-thorn and other extraordinary desert plants. The trail circles through a fantastic sculpture-garden of weathered quartz monzonite, then enters a shallow wash — notice how the vegetation changes in the slightly cooler and moister environment. The trail follows the wash past Skull Rock, then crosses the road and continues through more monzonite monoliths.

Follow the trail as it dips into several small arroyos and climbs across large granitic outcrops. Use caution if you attempt to scramble to the summit of any of these great, rounded outcrops — more than one hiker has found it easier to climb up than to climb down. Don't get stranded in an embarrassing situation. Take your time on this delightful trail; it'll soon have you back at the entrance to the Jumbo Rocks Campground.

MASTODON PEAK VIA MASTODON MINE TRAIL

DISTANCE: 3.2 miles round-trip

TRAILHEAD: Cottonwood Spring parking area

ELEVATION: Start 2995 feet; highest 3380 feet

GRADES: Moderate, with one steep section

RANGER STATION: Cottonwood Visitor Center

BEST SEASONS: Fall, winter or spring

PLANT COMMUNITIES: Desert riparian or stream-side; fan palm oasis

COMMON PLANTS: California fan palm, cottonwood, ocotillo, paper-bag bush, cat-claw acacia, jojoba, California juniper, Joshua tree, creosote bush, Mojave yucca, red-topped buckwheat, pencil cholla, Bigelow cholla

COMMON ANIMALS: spiny, whiptailed and zebra-tailed lizards, mourning dove, Scott's oriole, deer mouse, desert cottontail, coyote

NOTE: No reliable water on the trail — carry an ample supply; summer heat may make mid-day hiking uncomfortable, so plan your hike for cooler times or seasons

The **MASTODON MINE TRAIL** starts at the Cottonwood Spring parking area, then goes immediately to Cottonwood Spring, a delightful oasis complete with fan palms, cottonwoods, singing birds, running water, cattails and a feeling of respite from the intense desert heat. The trail climbs along a wash to the junction with the Lost Palms Trail — take the left fork for Mastodon Peak. The vegetation here is open and garden-like, with a great variety of desert plants. As the trail ascends the side of Mastodon Peak, it passes through an area that is again garden-like — this time reminding the hiker of a rock garden. When the trail crests the ridge below the summit of Mastodon Peak, take the short steep spur trail to the top (this may be too steep for some hikers). From there you have good views of the Coachella Valley, Ryan Mountain, Cottonwood Campground and the nearby desert landscape.

Return to the main trail, which descends to Mastodon Mine (a shaft, some wooden cribbing and a few rusting barrels). The trail then follows an old roadbed, dropping into a wash and passing the site of Winona Mill, with its eucalyptus trees, cottonwoods and a lone palm. You'll notice a small seep on the left side of the wash — this is a good place to look for birds, animal tracks and other signs of wildlife. As the trail leaves the wash and tops a small ridge, a branch trail to the right takes you to the campground, while the trail to the left returns to the Cottonwood Springs parking area.

If you have time, walk back down to the oasis — it's a wonderful place to sit and rest in the shade after hiking a few miles in Joshua Tree's lovely desert country.

Joshua Tree National Monument (NPS photo)

5

DEATH VALLEY
NATIONAL MONUMENT

Death Valley National Monument contains about 3000 square miles of prime desert and desert-mountan landscape — that's an area about the size of the states of Delaware and Rhode Island combined. The habitats represented in this far-flung national monument vary from salt pans (one, at 280 feet below sea level, is the lowest place in the New World) to sub-alpine environments on the summit of Telescope Peak (at a cool 11049 feet). As you might suspect, such great elevational differences lead to equally large changes in vegetation. The monument's vegetational zones include creosote bush, desert holly and mesquite communities at lower elevations; shadscale, blackbrush, Joshua tree and pinon-juniper communities at the middle elevations with limber pine and bristlecone pine woodlands in the highest mountains. Rainfall is scanty, varying from 1.68 inches in the driest valleys to a respectable 15 inches in the higher mountains surrounding the valley floor. Although the lowlands are almost bare of vegetation, where water is available plant life is abundant; in all, there are some 900 varieties of plants known from the monument. Whether you're interested in natural history, human history or both, you'll like hiking in Death Valley. Start with two of my favorites, the trails to Keane Wonder Mine and to

Telescope Peak, then try others on your own. You'll soon learn to love this vast monument of deserts and mountains.

GETTING THERE: Death Valley is east of US 395, via CA 178 or CA 190; US 95 is east of the monument and connects with NV 267, NV 374 and NV 373 to the monument. I-15 is southeast of the monument and connects with CA 127

ABOUT DAY-HIKING: Permits are not mandatory but it's highly recommended that you discuss your plans with rangers; special regulations apply in summer (contact Visitor Center, 619-786-2331, or any ranger station)

MONUMENT INFORMATION: Visitor Center (619-786-2331)

CAMPGROUNDS: Furnace Creek, Texas Spring, Sunset, Stove Pipe Wells, Emigrant, Mesquite Spring, Wildrose, Thorndike, Mahogany Flat, Pinyon Mesa

REPORT EMERGENCIES: Visitor Center (786-2331), any Ranger Station or any ranger

NEAREST PHYSICIAN: Lone Pine, California; Las Vegas, Nevada

MONUMENT ADDRESS: Death Valley National Monument, Death Valley, California 92328

WEATHER: Hot, hotter and hottest. Winter highs are in the 60s and 70s, while summer highs are well into the 100s. Humidity is, of course, low throughout the year.

KEANE WONDER MINE TRAIL

DISTANCE: 2 miles round-trip

TRAILHEAD: Keane Wonder Mill parking area (11 miles north of Furnace Creek, then 2 miles east)

ELEVATION: Start 1360 feet; highest 3120 feet

GRADES: Very steep, but not tiring if taken slowly

RANGER STATION: Furnace Creek Visitor Center

BEST SEASONS: Late fall through early spring

PLANT COMMUNITY: Creosote bush

COMMON PLANTS: Creosote bush, shadscale, desert trumpet

COMMON ANIMALS: Zebra-tailed lizard, side-blotched lizard, turkey vulture, raven

NOTE: There's no water along this trail — carry an ample supply; there may be open mineshafts in areas off the trail; summer heat may limit hiking to cooler hours

The **KEANE WONDER MINE TRAIL** begins on an old road at the end of the Keane Wonder Mine parking area. The mine and mill, perched on the western slopes of the Funeral Mountains, dates from the early 1900's. An aerial tramway moved gold, silver and lead ore from an ore-crusher to a mill where the material was concentrated; the minerals were then transported to Rhyolite, Nevada, for shipment by rail. To reach the headworks of the tramway, follow the roadbed a short distance, staying left at the junction with another old road descending to the right.

At the interpretive sign take the steeply ascending trail which levels out a bit in about a half-mile. Another half-mile takes you to the headworks of the aerial tramway which moved ore from the mine to the mill at the slope's base. The buckets of the tramway were loaded with crushed ore at the headworks, the force of the descending buckets powering an ore-crusher at the site. Take time to look at the clever engineering of the ore-crusher and tramway, but watch for open holes and areas of poor footing around the headworks.

As you descend to the parking area, you'll notice an old mine entrance about a quarter-mile down the trail from the headworks (it's nearly hidden to hikers ascending the trail). Glance inside if you wish, but don't enter the mine itself. Rather, notice the great views of Death Valley and the Panamint Mountains to the west and southwest as you descend.

TELESCOPE TRAIL TO ROGERS AND BENNETT PEAKS

DISTANCE: 3.5 miles one-way

TRAILHEAD: Mahogany Flat Campground

ELEVATION: Start 8200 feet; highest 9980 feet

GRADES: Moderate, with one slightly steeper section

RANGER STATION: Wildrose Ranger Station

BEST SEASONS: Spring, summer, winter

PLANT COMMUNITIES: Pinon pine, limber pine, subalpine sage meadow

COMMON PLANTS: Single-leaf pinon pine, sage, mountain mahogany, cliffrose, penstemon, Indian paintbrush, lupine

COMMON ANIMALS: Coyotes, burros, juncos, hummingbirds, ravens, mule deer, mountain cottontails

NOTE: No water is available along trail or at Mahagony Flat Campground — carry an ample supply from Wildrose Campground; some possibility of late afternoon thunderstorms and lightning; winter hikes may require special gear and a start from Charcoal Kilns, adding two miles to the hike

The **TELESCOPE PEAK TRAIL** to Rogers and Bennett Peaks starts in a pinon pine forest at the entrance to Mahogany Campground. This is a delightful hike for those wanting to escape the heat of the monument's lower elevations or wanting to sample the mountain environment surrounding Death Valley. Sign in at the trail register a few hundred yards up the trail; enjoy the fine views of Death Valley as you hike gradually upward.

The trail passes through an area with schist outcrops, then along open slopes with more good views of Death Valley and the Furnace Creek area. After about three miles of gradual climbing you'll enter a saddle between Rogers and Bennett Peaks. Notice that all the plants in the saddle are low-growing — a response to the nearly constant wind to which the plants are exposed. The view to the west from this point includes at least five ranges of mountains, with the Sierra Nevada dominating the western horizon. With luck, you'll be able to spot Mount Whitney on the skyline.

To reach the summit of Bennett Peak follow the trail to a second low saddle, then strike off cross-country. You'll pass through several stands of limber pines before reaching the highest point on Bennett Peak. Be prepared for some wind and cool temperatures here, even in the middle of the summer.

Return to the trail at the saddles, then hike cross-country again to reach the summit of Rogers Peak. As you climb the slope, you'll see the road from Mahogany Flat Campground climbing toward the summit. At the highest point the National Park Service maintains an antenna array, complete with diesel generator. After absorbing the fine views in all directions, you can return to the trailhead either by taking the road down or returning to the trail.

This is a most enjoyable hike, especially during the hotter months when you may want to escape to cooler elevations — you can save your low-elevation hiking for the morning and evening hours and enjoy this remarkable national monument in comfort.

6

LAKE MEAD NATIONAL RECREATION AREA

Lake Mead National Recreation Area is best known as a boater's playground, but there are attractive day-hikes for Seniors with the time and energy to find them. Most hikes follow either backcountry four-wheel-drive roads or washes. Colorful rock formations, brooding mountains set against the blue backdrop of the lake, undeciphered petroglyphs — all are worth the effort of getting a few miles off the main roads. Hiking is mainly cross-country, and best done during the cooler months. Lake Mead National Recreation Area can be hot and dry at almost any season, so be sure to carry sufficient water, and to inform a reliable friend of your destination and return time. There's one day-hike I especially enjoy — I hope you'll like it, too.

GETTING THERE: From Las Vegas take US 93 to Boulder City and Hoover Dam; the Alan Bible Visitor Center is mid-way between Boulder City and the dam. If coming from Kingman and I-40, take US 93 to Hoover Dam; the visitor center is 3 miles north of the dam.

ABOUT DAY-HIKING: Permits are not mandatory, but it's suggested that you inform rangers at the closest ranger station or visitor center of your plans

NATIONAL RECREATION AREA INFORMATION: Alan Bible Visitor Center or any of the eight District Ranger Stations, or call 702-293-4041

CAMPGROUNDS: Boulder Beach, Las Vegas Wash, Callville Bay, Echo Bay, Overton Beach (no fee), Temple Bar, Cottonwood Cove, Katherine

REPORT EMERGENCIES: Alan Bible Visitor Center, District Ranger Stations (associated with campgrounds), or any ranger; call 702-293-4041

NEAREST PHYSICIAN: Boulder City, Nevada; Overton, Nevada; Bullhead City, Arizona; Henderson, Nevada

NATIONAL RECREATION AREA ADDRESS: Lake Mead National Recreation Area, 601 Nevada Highway, Boulder City, Nevada 89005

WEATHER: Summer highs usually over 100. Fall, winter and spring temperatures are less extreme, with winter highs in the 50s and winter nightly lows seldom below freezing. Humidity is low; most rain comes in July, August and September; only 4 inches per year, but there may be some danger of local flash flooding.

COHENOUR MINE TRAIL

DISTANCE: 4.0 miles one-way

TRAILHEAD: Junction of roads to Bonelli Landing and Detrital Bay (on Temple Bar access road, 15 miles southeast of Hoover Dam on US 93)

ELEVATION: Start 1600 feet; highest 3000 feet

GRADES: Very easy

RANGER STATION: Temple Bar District Ranger Station

BEST SEASONS: Fall, winter, spring

PLANT COMMUNITY: Creosote bush

COMMON PLANTS: Creosote bush, mesquite, mistletoe, prickly pear, blackbush, brittlebush, mormon tea, barrel cactus, Joshua tree

COMMON ANIMALS: Burro, mourning dove, western kingbird, blacktailed jackrabbit, desert cottontail, whiptail lizard, harvester ant, desert bighorn in mountains and canyons

NOTE: No water sources along the trail — carry an ample supply; extreme heat and solar radiation may be problems at any season

The **COHENOUR MINE TRAIL,** marked as "Road 71", begins in a creosote bush flat two miles south of Bonelli Landing Primitive Campground, at the junction of the dirt roads leading to Bonelli Landing and Detrital Bay. The Bonelli Landing Road (Road 74) is approached from the Temple Bar Access Road, which joins US 93 fifteen miles southeast of Hoover Dam. The trail to Cohenour Mine soon leaves the valley bottom to rise gently across a series of low ridges covered with a gravelly desert pavement and creosote bush. There are good views of the Black Mountains, the Gale Hills and the Muddy Mountains along the first part of the trail. The Black Mountains are the home of one of the largest populations of desert bighorn in the Southwest, and the sheep's tracks and droppings can usually be found where the trail wanders through several canyons.

In about two miles the trail enters a major wash, goes past a backcountry campsite, and divides at the upper end of a narrow canyon. Take the left fork where the major canyon ends. Look for petroglyphs pecked into the rocks in the area of the backcountry campsite and all along the canyon walls in this area. The trail enters a wide canyon with columnar-jointed cliffs; follow the trail to the next junction, where the left fork will take you to the Pope Mine and the right fork to the site of the Cohenour Mine. Whichever route you take, watch for open prospect holes and uncovered shafts in areas off the trail. There is an old Spanish arrastra or ore-crusher as well as more petroglyphs near the trail to the Pope Mine; specific directions to these can be given by the rangers at Temple Bar.

To return to your vehicle, retrace your route but avoid taking short-cuts. There are fine views of the Virgin Basin and Temple Basin areas of Lake Mead to be enjoyed as you hike back to the main road.

7

ORGAN PIPE CACTUS NATIONAL MONUMENT

Organ Pipe Cactus National Monument protects the rare organ pipe cactus and preserves a segment of the far-flung Sonoran Desert. Organ Pipe Cactus National Monument has something for every desert hiker, whether novice or expert. The variety seems endless, with rugged dry mountain ranges, bajadas or outwash plains which seem to reach beyond the horizon, vast creosote bush flats and intimate dry washes or arroyos. The land appears harsh and uninhabitable to the casual visitor, but the Senior hiker who takes time to understand the area finds an abundance of life. Situated on the Arizona-Sonora border, the monument is home for a number of plants and animals which are usually found only in Mexico. If you're a birdwatcher, you'll want to spend some time at Quitobaquito Spring or waiting quietly at one of the tanks or water-holes — perhaps the ones in Alamo Canyon. While there aren't many formal trails in the monument (nearly all of it is accessible but undeveloped backcountry), two that I particularly enjoy are the Alamo Canyon hike and the Victoria Mine Trail. I think you'll enjoy them, too.

GETTING THERE: Organ Pipe Cactus National Monument is 140 miles south of Phoenix (via US 80 and AZ 85) or 142 miles southwest of Tucson (via AZ 86 and AZ 85); if coming from Mexico, the monument is approached via Route 2 (from the west) or Routes 2 and 8 (from the south)

ABOUT DAY-HIKING: No permits are needed, but you should notify responsible friends of your route and return time

MONUMENT INFORMATION: Visitor Center (602-387-6849)

CAMPGROUNDS: Campground (1.3 miles south of Visitor Center); Alamo Canyon Primitive Campground (tents only; 14 miles north of Visitor Center; required permits are available at the Visitor Center)

REPORT EMERGENCIES: Visitor Center (387-6849), Campground Ranger Station or any ranger

NEAREST PHYSICIAN: Phoenix or Tucson, Arizona

MONUMENT ADDRESS: Organ Pipe Cactus National Monument, Route 1, Box 100, Ajo, Arizona 85321

WEATHER: Hot, dry summers, with less than nine inches of rain annually, half falling as gentle winter rains. Summer thunderstorms are extremely local and of short duration, but may bring a danger of flash flooding. Winters are generally warm and mild, with few nights having freezing temperatures.

VICTORIA MINE TRAIL

DISTANCE: 2.2 miles one-way

TRAILHEAD: RV dump station at far end of campground

ELEVATION: Start 1680 feet; highest 1680 feet

GRADES: Easy

RANGER STATIONS: Campground; Visitor Center

BEST SEASONS: November through April

PLANT COMMUNITY: Mixed cactus-palo verde

COMMON PLANTS: Saguaro, ocotillo, palo verde, creosote bush, mesquite

COMMON ANIMALS: Desert cottontail, blacktail jackrabbit, antelope squirrel, spiny lizard, whiptail lizard, cardinal, cactus wren, desert sparrow, mourning dove, curve-billed thrasher, phainopepla; collared peccary are also found in this area, but seldom seen

NOTE: No water sources along the trail — carry an ample supply of water; areas off the trail may have open mineshafts — stay on or near the trail

The **VICTORIA MINE TRAIL** begins at the campground's RV dump station (far southern end of the campground). Sign the trail register at the trailhead, then take the well-marked path through creosote bush, chainfruit cholla, and scattered saguaros. The trail goes generally south and southwest across rolling terrain, shallow washes and low ridges. As you hike the first section of the trail, watch for palo verde "nurse-trees" with young saguaros growing up through the tree's branches, and for tracks of the collared peccary in the sand of the arroyo-bottoms. From the low ridges you'll have good views of the Ajo Mountains to the northeast, the small Mexican community of Sonoita to the south, and of the dry but impressive Cubabi Mountains still further south in Sonora. There are benches in the cool shade of the well-vegetated washes where you can rest and watch dozens of species of desert birds, or simply enjoy the peaceful surroundings while catching your breath.

The trail joins an old jeep road after about two miles; follow the sign and go left on the road for a few hundred yards to the site of the Victoria Mine. This is a fascinating place, with what was probably the company store, rusting mining machinery, old tools and other debris left when the mine was abandoned. Use care, though, as you explore — there may be a few open mineshafts left in the area.

Retrace your route to return to the campground, and enjoy the good views of the Ajo Mountains and of Twin Peaks. Spend a moment, too, savoring the quiet desert or listening for the music of the wind moving gently through a saguaro's spines — this is a trail that encourages the Senior hiker to enjoy such things.

ALAMO CANYON HIKE

DISTANCE: 1.6 miles one-way

TRAILHEAD: Alamo Canyon Primitive Campground (take AZ 85 ten miles north from Visitor Center, then go four miles east on a well-maintained dirt road)

ELEVATION: Start 2266 feet; highest 2800 feet

GRADES: Moderate, but with one short steep section

RANGER STATION: Visitor Center

BEST SEASONS: November through April

PLANT COMMUNITY: Evergreen woodland

COMMON PLANTS: Junipers, Ajo oak, mulberry, netleaf hackberry, rosewood, catclaw acacia, desert broom

COMMON ANIMALS: Cardinal, mourning dove, canyon wren, various hummingbirds, coyote, spiny lizard, whiptail lizard, serpulid wasp; you may also be lucky enough to see desert bighorn sheep, whitetail deer and collared peccary

NOTE: Surface water is unsafe — take ample supply of good water; some scrambling required; thorny vegetation off main route

The **ALAMO CANYON HIKE** begins on an old road in the wash just below the Alamo Canyon Primitive Campground. Hike down this road, passing the remains of two old buildings and through an old corral. The plants along this section are typical of the Sonoran Desert foothills — saguaro, organ pipe cactus, ocotillo, creosote bush and teddybear cholla. It's an impressive landscape with beautiful desert mountains and cliffs rising from the canyon's edge.

Walk through the corral and past a burnt-adobe water tank, then follow the wash upstream less than a hundred yards where you'll see a smaller wash entering from your right. Follow this smaller wash through patches of dense vegetation (it's easiest to walk right in the center of the wash, rather than along the slopes on either side). After a few hundred yards the wash's bed becomes nearly free of vegetation, making hiking much easier. Stay in the wash — don't take any of the side-canyons which enter the valley.

About a mile upstream the wash is blocked by large boulders which form a waterfall when the creek is running — for most hikers the trail will end here. More adventurous Seniors can go a few yards downstream from the boulder dam and find a way to scramble to the low saddle on the left of the "waterfall". A scramble over the low saddle will bring you to a series of small tinajas or pools frequented by desert bighorn, mourning doves and other animals attracted to the nearly constant water supply. Take time to look for bighorn sheep on the nearby cliffs and to observe animal tracks around the pools. You'll enjoy the abundant bird-life in the area, too.

To return to the trailhead, retrace your route through the wash. Be sure to take your camera on this hike — there's a fair chance you'll be able to photograph desert bighorn sheep as they watch you from the nearby ridges.

8

SAGUARO NATIONAL MONUMENT

Saguaro National Monument was established to protect two small but important samples of the great Sonoran Desert, including superb stands of the saguaro or giant cactus. The monument is in two sections, both very near the city of Tucson — the eastern section centers around the high Rincon Mountains, while the western unit includes some of the least-modified areas of the Tucson Mountains. Both contain fine and easily accessible stands of saguaro, as well as prime representatives of the upland desert plant community. The trail system of the Rincon Mountains unit is quite extensive, with trails taking the hiker from the edge of Tucson (at 2700 feet) to the top of Mica Mountain (8666 feet) — and through at least six major types of vegetation on the way. The Tucson Mountains Unit has fewer trails but is just as interesting to the Senior hiker. There are two trails, one in each unit of the monument, that I've particularly enjoyed hiking — I think you'll like them, too.

GETTING THERE: Both units of the monument are quite near Tucson — just follow the signs directing you to the monument from anywhere in town

ABOUT DAY-HIKING: Permits are not mandatory, but you may inform rangers at the Visitor Center (Rincon Mountains Unit) or Information Center (Tucson Mountains Unit) of your plans

MONUMENT INFORMATION: Visitor Center or Information Center (602-296-8576)

CAMPGROUNDS: None in the monument itself other than backcountry sites — there are a number of Forest Service and private campgrounds in the area, and Tucson Mountain Park has a campground located four miles south of the Tucson Mountain Unit

REPORT EMERGENCIES: Visitor Center, Information Center or by calling 911

NEAREST PHYSICIAN: Tucson, Arizona

MONUMENT ADDRESS: Saguaro National Monument, Old Spanish Trail, Route 8, Box 695, Tucson, Arizona 85730

WEATHER: Winter temperatures are usually mild with daily highs often over 65. Summer highs are often over 100. Rainfall is scanty (11 inches annually), with summer thunderstorms and gentle winter rains

DOUGLAS SPRING TRAIL

DISTANCE: 5.1 miles one-way

TRAILHEAD: End of Tucson's East Speedway Boulevard (Rincon Mountains Unit)

ELEVATION: Start 2700 feet; highest 4850 feet

GRADES: Easy to moderate

RANGER STATION: Visitor Center (Rincon Mountain Unit)

BEST SEASONS: Fall, winter and spring

PLANT COMMUNITIES: Sonoran Desert Lifezone (upland desert)

COMMON PLANTS: Saguaro, creosote bush, manzanita, oaks, cholla, prickly pear cactus

COMMON ANIMALS: Desert cottontail, blacktail jackrabbit, collared peccary, whitetailed and mule deer, Gambel's quail, mourning dove, cactus wren, cardinal, pyrrhuloxia, whiptail lizard, spiny lizards, collared lizard

NOTE: No reliable water along trail — carry a full canteen; summer heat may make hiking early or late advisable; some loose stones on the trail; take care to lock your vehicle at this trailhead

The **DOUGLAS SPRING TRAIL** starts at a well-marked trailhead at the east end of Tucson's Speedway Boulevard. The trail winds through a fine community of creosote bush, palo verdes, mesquites, chollas, prickly pears and mature saguaro cacti. The lower parts of the trail go through good bird habitat; the birds are especially active at dawn and dusk, making early or late hikes even more enjoyable. The first half-mile is gently rolling, passing through a mature saguaro forest and several small washes.

The trail then climbs a moderate grade along a small ridge, giving good views of Tucson and the Santa Catalina

Mountains north of the city. The trail soon turns toward the southeast and continues to climb toward a small saddle. As the ridge is topped, notice an impressive wash on your left and the presence of younger (but fewer) saguaros in this area, and the many ocotillos. The trail passes an old fence-line from the pre-park days when the area was used extensively for ranching. After crossing another low saddle the path drops into a wash (watch for deer here), and follows the southwest side of a hill. In another quarter-mile the trail crosses yet another wash; this is a good place to observe both birds and aquatic life when pools are present. The trail pulls away from the wash, passing through an area with abundant jojoba plants. The trail becomes nearly level as it tops a broad ridge and trends east along a mesquite-lined wash. If the time of day is right, notice the flow of cooler air in the wash and the movement of air along the warmer slopes.

The trail then crosses another small wash lined with juniper and coyote willow, then climbs steeply and enters an area of oaks, juniper and grasses. Again there are excellent views of Tucson and the Santa Catalinas, as well as an impressive wash with extensive areas of exposed bedrock to your right. The grade moderates after a short climb, bringing you to an area of oak, shin-dagger, pinon pine and grasses — a very pretty site. The trail follows dry washes for the last mile, then comes to the Douglas Spring backcountry campsites. The campsites themselves are along the edges of a dry streambed lined with dense vegetation. There's a pit toilet at the site, but the spring can't be counted on as a water source.

Retrace your route to the trailhead, enjoying impressive views of the city of Tucson and its surrounding mountains.

SENDERO ESPERANZA-KING CANYON TRAIL

DISTANCE: 4.0 miles one-way (8.0 if no shuttle can be arranged)

TRAILHEAD: Sendero Esperanza Trailhead (on Golden Gate Road in the Tucson Mountains Unit)

ELEVATION: Start 2980 feet; highest 3600 feet

GRADES: Easy (one short steep section)

RANGER STATION: Red Hills Information Center

BEST SEASONS: Late fall through early spring

PLANT COMMUNITY: Upland desert

COMMON PLANTS: Saguaro, palo verde, mesquite, ocotillo, yucca, cane cholla, beavertail prickly pear

COMMON ANIMALS: Mourning dove, gambel's quail, gila woodpecker, northern flicker, cactus wren, spiny lizard, whiptail lizard, desert cottontail, blacktail jackrabbit, velvet ant

NOTE: No water on trail — take plenty with you; lock your vehicle at this trailhead

The **SENDERO ESPERANZA-KING CANYON TRAIL** starts in a lovely desert garden of palo verdes, saguaros and mesquites. The trail follows an old road for the first three-quarters of a mile, crossing several minor washes and a major one as it nears the base of the hills. The trail in this section is wide and nearly level, going through an excellent example of upland desert vegetation. The trail climbs through a series of easy switchbacks, generally paralleling the course of a major wash. Look for old prospect holes as the trail climbs — reminders of early-day mining activity.

An easy grade takes you to a trail junction on a low saddle. The view north is of the desert bajada you've just crossed, with the northern portion of the Avra Valley stretching beyond. To the south you can see the southern reaches of the same valley, and Kitt Peak and distant desert mountain ranges along the Mexican border; near the base of the nearby hills is the Arizona-Sonora Desert Museum — very close to your destination.

A series of switchbacks descends from the saddle and soon joins another old road. The trail goes through more fine stands of saguaro, younger in age than those of the Rincon Mountains area. The trail is on an old roadbed which is being naturally reclaimed by grasses. It descends past Gould Mine — the shaft of which has several active beehives (another good reason to stay out of old mines). Like most mines in the area, the Gould was located for its traces of silver and gold, but the most valuable mineral taken was copper. The roofless building was apparently the mine's powder-house. The trail passes another old road and crosses a wash — stay on the main trail which takes you to the Mam-A-Gah picnic area.

At the trail junction take the trail marked "Desert Museum". Your route will cross King Canyon wash on an exposed bedrock "step"; while there is seldom water in the wash, you can usually find moist sand by digging a shallow pit in the wash's bed. As you near the end of the King Canyon Trail, there are good views of King Canyon itself and of Wasson Peak, the highest point in the Tucson Mountains. A few minutes walk takes you to the King Canyon trailhead.

You can return to the Sendero Esperanza trailhead by retracing your hike, by trying to catch a ride to your vehicle, or by arranging a car-shuttle with your hiking partner.

This trail offers a good introduction to desert hiking — especially if it's made as part of a visit to the Arizona-Sonora Desert Museum.

Sequoia National Park   (NPS photo)

Pinnacles National Monument   (NPS photo)

9

CHIRICAHUA
NATIONAL MONUMENT

Chiricahua National Monument is a forested island in a sea of desert grasslands, cool and inviting after the lowland's heat. Millions of years ago a series of explosive volcanic eruptions laid down layers of hot ash. This ash became welded into rock; over the eons, the layers of welded volcanic material eroded into a wonderland of pillars, balanced rocks, soft cliffs and deep valleys. As the climate grew warmer and drier, the Chiricahua Mountains became a haven for plants and animals that could only survive in cooler, more moist conditions. Part of the monument's attraction is the vivid contrast between cool, inviting highlands and the hot, arid lands shimmering below. Add the monument's fantastically weathered rock formations and you have the makings of a truly unique hiking experience. More than seventeen miles of trails lead to unusual and interesting destinations. The Senior hiker can easily discover cool, shady glens on the Echo Canyon Trail, or get inspiring views of the mountains and valleys of southeastern Arizona by taking a short hike to the summit of Sugarloaf Mountain.

GETTING THERE: The monument can be approached from I-10 at Bowie (via a county road) or Willcox (via US 186), or from Douglas (via US 666 and AZ 181)

ABOUT DAY-HIKING: Permits aren't mandatory, but you may inform rangers at the Visitor Center of your plans

MONUMENT INFORMATION: Visitor Center (602-824-3560)

CAMPGROUNDS: Bonita Canyon Campground (half mile from Visitor Center)

REPORT EMERGENCIES: Visitor Center (824-3560) or to any ranger (after business hours call the numbers posted on bulletin boards at the Visitor Center or campground)

NEAREST PHYSICIAN: Willcox, Arizona

MONUMENT ADDRESS: Chiricahua National Monument, Dos Cabezas Route, Box 6500, Willcox, Arizona 85643

WEATHER: Temperatures are moderate; the January mean is 40, while the July mean is only 74. Anticipate afternoon thunderstorms during the summer months.

SUGARLOAF MOUNTAIN TRAIL

DISTANCE: 2.0 miles round-trip

TRAILHEAD: Sugarloaf Parking Area (just off Bonita Canyon Road)

ELEVATION: Start 6800 feet; highest 7308 feet

GRADES: Easy to moderate

RANGER STATION: Visitor Center

BEST SEASONS: Spring, summer, or fall

PLANT COMMUNITY: Oak-juniper forest

COMMON PLANTS: Manzanita, madrone, scrub oak, yucca, agave, cacti

COMMON ANIMALS: Blacktail jackrabbit, antelope squirrel, coatimundi, whitetail and mule deer, gray-breasted jay, plain and bridled titmouse, spiny lizard, whiptail lizard

NOTE: No water sources along this trail — take an ample supply; lightning hazard at summit during thunderstorms

The **SUGARLOAF MOUNTAIN TRAIL** begins at a parking area near the end of the six-and-a-half mile scenic drive from the Visitor Center to Massai Point. The destination of the hike, a fire lookout at the summit of Sugarloaf Mountain, can be seen from the road and parking area, and it looks like a forbidding climb. Take heart, though — the hike is much less demanding than it appears.

The trail climbs gently through manzanita stands, past an isolated Arizona cypress or two, then through cuts in rhyolite formations, giving a closeup of the structure of the rock which makes up most of the impressive formations preserved in the monument. In fact, the trail goes through a ridge of rhyolite — the only way to maintain a reasonable gradient was to hack a tunnel through the rock.

As the trail spirals around Sugarloaf Mountain, note the differences in vegetation on north-facing and south-facing slopes. The south-facing slopes are hotter and drier, while the north-facing hillsides are cooler and more moist; one hillside supports plants of the true desert, while the other has plants usually found further north or at higher elevations.

The trail goes through a burned area as it nears the summit — a beautiful place with skeletons of manzanita underlain by a profusion of colorful low-growing ground cover. The fire lookout at the summit offers a scenic circle of desert and mountains — Cochise Head to the north, Dos Cabezas Peak to the northwest, Sulpher Spring Valley and the Willcox Playa to the west, the Huachuca Mountains to the southwest, Echo Canyon with its extensive rhyolite "organ pipe" formations to the south, and the San Simon Valley to the east completes the circle. The lookout is used to monitor lightning strikes during summer thunderstorms, so be appropriately cautioned and time your hike to arrive at the summit well before the usual summer-afternoon buildup of cumulus thunderheads.

This is a delightful trail, rewarding the Senior hiker with great views of the monument and its surrounding mountains and valleys. From the summit you can look down on your vehicle, waiting as you retrace your steps to return to the parking area.

ECHO CANYON LOOP

DISTANCE: 3.5 miles round-trip

TRAILHEAD: Echo Park Parking Area (on Bonita Canyon Road)

ELEVATION: Start 6750 feet; midway 6250 feet; highest 6750 feet

GRADES: Easy to moderate

RANGER STATION: Visitor Center

BEST SEASONS: Spring, summer or fall

PLANT COMMUNITIES: Oak-juniper-pinon pine forest; riparian or streamside forest

COMMON PLANTS: Apache pine, Arizona cypress, Chihuhua pine, madrone, manzanita

COMMON ANIMALS: White-tailed and mule deer, coatimundi, peccary, spiny and whiptail lizards, canyon wren, steller's jay, Scott's oriole

NOTE: Water sources are unreliable — carry a full canteen; you may find an occassional loose rock on the trail

The **ECHO CANYON LOOP TRAIL** starts in a delightful garden of manzanita, alligator junipers and pinon pines. The trail goes immediately through a small clearing — take the most obvious pathway, the one directly across from your entrance to the clearing. At the trail junction a hundred yards from the clearing, follow the sign for "Echo Park". Note the madrone, pinon pines, Chihuhua pines and narrowleaf manzanita in this area, as well as the silverleaf and netleaf oaks.

The trail follows a southwest-trending ridge with good views of Sugarloaf Mountain and Cochise Head. As the trail gradually descends, you'll hike past several fine examples of Arizona cypress and have good views of the rhyolite pillars forming cliffs at the base of Sugarloaf Mountain.

After going through a series of rhyolite towers, the trail enters Echo Park itself, an island of coolness crowded with large trees and echoing with bird-song. You can record your successful descent at a trail register beside the path.

The trail wanders through dense riparian forest, then follows a small intermittant stream. Note the Douglas firs beside the trail; their distinctive cones litter the forest floor, a reminder of the cool and moist environment of the canyon. The trail follows the valley, staying level as the canyon drops away below it, then turns and follows a hotter south-facing slope; note the distinct change in vegetation as the trail gradually climbs the warmer hillside.

Stay on the left fork at the trail junction midway up the slope. Soon there are beautiful views of the heavy vegetation in upper Rhyolite Canyon. At the next trail junction, again take the left trail (marked "Echo Canyon Parking Area"). The trail once more parallels a dry streambed, reaching yet another trail junction — as usual, take the route marked "Echo Canyon Parking Area". The path climbs a bit more steeply here, but soon brings you back to your vehicle.

I think you'll enjoy this trail — it's a beauty, especially during the spring and fall.

10

CORONADO NATIONAL MEMORIAL

Coronado National Memorial commemorates the first major intrusion of Europeans into the American Southwest. Set in the Huachuca Mountains, Montezuma Canyon gives the Senior hiker a good introduction to the Mexican oak-pinon woodland, as well as offering sweeping overviews of a portion of the route followed by Coronado and his party of explorers. Hikers in Montezuma Canyon get a good idea of the difficulties encountered by Coronado's men as they followed the San Pedro Valley in their search for the Cities of Gold. Besides being an important historic monument, Coronado National Memorial is a place of unusual plant and animal life. Among the birds, for instance, the coppery-tailed trogon, rufous-crowned sparrow, Mexican jay and many other rare or unusual species are all found in the area's canyons and woodlands. Take time to sit quietly on a hillside and enjoy this beautiful place — it'll be time well-spent.

GETTING THERE: The memorial is 50 miles south of I-10, or 20 miles south of Sierra Vista off AZ 92; the Montezuma Canyon Road which leads to the memorial joins State 92 about 25 miles west of Bisbee.

ABOUT DAY-HIKING: No permit is needed, but hikers are encouraged to check in with rangers at the visitor center

MEMORIAL INFORMATION: Visitor Center (602-458-9333 during business hours, 366-5515 at other times)

CAMPGROUNDS: None in memorial or in adjacent national forest

REPORT EMERGENCIES: Visitor Center (458-9333 or 366-5515) or any ranger

NEAREST PHYSICIAN: Sierra Vista or Bisbee, Arizona

MEMORIAL ADDRESS: Coronado National Memorial, RR 2, Box 126, Hereford, Arizona 85615

WEATHER: Summer days are hot to very hot (upper 90s), but the humidity is comfortably low. Winter highs are in the 40-60 range with freezing temperatures at night. Late June through early September is the rainy season, with afternoon thunderstorms and lightning common. Winter months may bring an occassional light snowfall. Annual precipitation is between 15 and 20 inches.

JOE'S CANYON TRAIL

DISTANCE: 3.1 miles one-way (add 0.3 miles for assent of Coronado Peak)

TRAILHEAD: Junction of Montezuma Canyon Road and picnic area entrance road (just west of Visitor Center)

ELEVATION: Start 5380 feet; highest 6575 feet

GRADES: Easy to moderate

RANGER STATION: Visitor Center

BEST SEASONS: Spring or fall

PLANT COMMUNITY: Mexican oak-pinon woodland

COMMON PLANTS: Mexican blue oaks, alligator juniper, Mexican pinon pine, sacahuista or bear-grass

COMMON ANIMALS: Turkey vulture, gray-breasted jay, scrub jay, coatimundi, peccary, white-tailed deer, spiny lizard, tree lizard

NOTE: No water along trail — carry an ample supply; summer heat; lightning during thunderstorms

The **JOE'S CANYON TRAIL** begins at the junction of the main road and the picnic area's entrance road, wanders uphill through oak-manzanita chaparral with cholla, sacahuista and pinon pines lining the path. The trail climbs gradually through a series of switchbacks, passing impressive agave or century plants; there are scattered oaks of several species on the hillsides.

About a mile and a half from the top, the trail passes along the base of a small cliff, but straightens as the grade moderates. You then hike along a beautiful grassy hillside dotted with oak, junipers, and pinon pines. The trail tops out on a grassy parklike saddle, then contours along the hillsides until the shelter atop Coronado Peak comes into sight. The trail levels out, giving you some good views into Montezuma Canyon and into the Mexican state of Sonora, less than a half-mile to the south.

The Joe's Canyon Trail intersects the Coronado Peak Trail; if you have time, take the short Coronado Peak Trail. You'll enjoy the view from the summit of Coronado Peak; take time to read the selections from the Coronado Expedition's journals quoted on interpretive markers beside the trail.

Signs direct you from the junction of the Joe's Canyon Trail and the Coronado Peak Trail to the red-roofed shelter on the main road. You can either walk down the road or retrace your route through Joe's Canyon to the picnic area and your vehicle.

Coronado National Memorial (NPS photo)

11

GRAND CANYON NATIONAL PARK

When one thinks of a national park, the Grand Canyon invariably comes to mind. It's truly awesome — deep and vast, constantly changing as light and shadow play on the spectacular walls and cliffs. Even the statistics, impressive as they are, give only the barest idea of the canyon's majesty. The gorge is about a mile deep, while the rim-to-rim distance ranges from only 600 feet to about 18 miles. The Colorado River travels some 277 miles through the canyon, moving silt, sand and gigantic boulders as the canyon continues to deepen. Smaller side canyons, each a miracle in itself, add to the beauty and grandeur of the main canyon. So important is the Grand Canyon that it has been given World Heritage Site status as a place of universal significance to be protected as part of mankind's common legacy. No matter how large or important the Grand Canyon is, though, it can still be an intimate place — especially if you take time to hike its trails. You'll find its majesty has a human scale when you walk among its wonders.

GETTING THERE: Grand Canyon's south rim is usually approached from Flagstaff (via US 180) or Williams (via AZ 64 and US 180), or from the east via US 160, US 89 and AZ 64

ABOUT DAY-HIKING: No permit is needed for day-hikes; if concerned about your hike, check with the Back-country Reservation Office (602-638-2474) for information

PARK INFORMATION: Any visitor center, or by calling 638-7888; call 638-9304 for a recorded message

CAMPGROUNDS: Mather Campground, located at Grand Canyon Village (reservations available through Ticketron); Trailer Village Campground at Grand Canyon Village (hookups available for RVs); Desert View Campground at Desert View; North Rim Campground at Bright Angel Point on the North Rim. Forest Service and commercial campgrounds are nearby but outside the park

REPORT EMERGENCIES: Any visitor center, ranger station, lodge, museum, or any park employee — or by calling 638-2477

NEAREST PHYSICIAN: Grand Canyon Clinic (Grand Canyon Village, call 638-2551)

PARK ADDRESS: Grand Canyon National Park, Box 129, Grand Canyon, Arizona 86023

WEATHER: South Rim is mild in summer, with highs in 80s or above. North Rim is much cooler, with summer maximums in 70s and 80s. Expect afternoon thundershowers on both North and South Rims during late summer. Temperatures within the canyon itself are much higher, with summer highs often above 115. While the North Rim is closed in winter, the South Rim is open, but expect cool to cold temperatures and some snow.

WEST RIM NATURE TRAIL

DISTANCE: 8.0 miles one-way (Mather Point to Hermit's Rest)

TRAILHEAD: Mather Point (return to your trailhead by shuttlebus during the summer season)

ELEVATION: Start 7129 feet; end 6789 feet; highest 7129 feet

GRADES: Very easy with one moderate section

RANGER STATIONS: Visitor Center, Yavapai Museum

BEST SEASONS: Year-round

PLANT COMMUNITY: Pinon pine-juniper woodland

COMMON PLANTS: Pinon pine, juniper, Douglas fir (seen in pockets just below the rim), Gambel's oak, ponderosa pine, mormon tea, sage, cliffrose, yucca, mountain mahogany

COMMON ANIMALS: Rock squirrel, cliff chipmunk, coyote, Abert squirrel, mule deer, raven, swift

NOTE: Several developed areas are near the trail; carry a canteen; sheer cliff faces adjacent to pathway — stay on trail

The **WEST RIM NATURE TRAIL** begins at Mather Point and follows the edge of the Grand Canyon to Hermit's Rest — a distance of eight miles. Since the trail passes several overlooks and developed areas it's possible to enjoy shorter portions of the hike if time is a problem. During the summer months a shuttlebus runs along West Rim Drive between Hermit's Rest and Yavapai Point. If you tire you can catch the shuttlebus at any of several designated overlooks along the trail.

The path wanders close to the canyon's edge, presenting constantly changing views of the canyon, glimpses of the Colorado River, and an intimate look at the plant and animal communities along the rim. Watch for Abert squirrels in the nearby ponderosa pine forest, for ravens and swifts gliding and swooping along the canyon's edge, and for signs of mule deer and coyotes all along the trail. Certainly you'll see many cliff chipmunks and rock squirrels. Remember that they're wild animals and shouldn't be fed or approached too closely.

The route passes through or close to a number of overlooks, each with interpretive information — take time to enjoy the views from each overlook and to read the information presented there. Within a few miles you'll have a good idea of how the canyon was formed and some insights into the human history of the area. You can make the hike as short or long as you wish, returning to your vehicle either by trail or by shuttlebus. I think you'll find this trail a good introduction to the canyon — it's certianly a beautiful place to start.

CEDAR RIDGE VIA SOUTH KAIBAB TRAIL

DISTANCE: 1.4 miles one-way

TRAILHEAD: South Kaibab Trailhead (on East Rim Drive)

ELEVATION: Start 7170 feet; end 5800 feet; highest 7170 feet

GRADES: Several steep sections, remainder moderately steep

RANGER STATION: Visitor Center, Yavapai Museum

BEST SEASONS: Spring, summer, fall

PLANT COMMUNITIES: Pinon pine-juniper forest, Douglas fir forest, upland desert grassland

COMMON PLANTS: Pinon pine, juniper, Douglas fir in pockets just below the canyon's rim, cliffrose, yucca, mormon tea, mountain mahogany

COMMON ANIMALS: Ravens, swifts, spiny lizard, rock squirrel, cliff chipmunk

NOTE: No water is available along the trail — carry an ample supply; summer heat may make early or late hiking necessary; there are some steep and rocky sections of trail; mule traffic also uses this trail; comfortable, sturdy shoes and a hat are recommended

The section of the **SOUTH KAIBAB TRAIL** between the rim and Cedar Ridge also offers a good introduction to hiking within the Grand Canyon. From the trailhead the route drops quickly through a series of switchbacks, passing from pinon pine-juniper woodland to a cooler, more moist ledge supporting a fine growth of Douglas fir (visible on the left in a damper side-canyon).

As the trail descends further, it enters a rocky and much warmer area — an upland desert grassland. The trail follows the general trend of Cedar Ridge, passing through four distinct rock layers, each older than the layer above. In order, these are the Kaibab, Toroweap, Coconino and Hermit Formations. Each represents about 10 million years of deposition. As you hike, notice the fossils exposed where the rock layers have eroded. (Like all other features of the national parks, the fossils are protected by law — leave them for others to enjoy.) If you continued your hike into the depths of the canyon, you'd pass through successive bands of sedementary deposits, each with its distinctive fossil flora and fauna. You can learn more about the geologic history of the canyon at the nearby fossil exhibit.

If you only have a short time and can't hike deeper into the canyon, a good place to turn around is at the chemical toilet on Cedar Ridge. If you should meet a mule train while hiking, move quietly to the uphill side of the trail and remain still until the mules have passed.

On your way back to the rim, hike slowly enough to enjoy the views of the Inner Gorge, the North Rim and the side canyons, and plan your next visit to the Grand Canyon — it's a magical place and people tend to come back to it again and again. So will you.

12

WUPATKI NATIONAL MONUMENT

Wupatki National Monument is primarily known for its archaeological sites. Some 2000 have been found so far, ranging from simple field markers to elaborate dwellings and villages. Apparently three distinct cultures, Kayenta Anasazi, Sinagua and Cohonina, shared the area some 800 years ago, trading both goods and ideas. The volcanic eruptions at nearby Sunset Crater spread a volcanic ash that was fertile and held water, making the Wupatki area attractive to dry-land farmers. Today the Senior hiker can sample a landscape that must look very much as it did 800 years ago, when Wupatki was the crossroads of ancient cultures. The landscape looks dry and sere, but I think you'll be surprised at how attractive it becomes when seen close-up.

GETTING THERE: From Flagstaff and I-40, take US 89 north, then a loop road to both Sunset and Wupatki National Monuments. If coming from Grand Canyon's east entrance, take US 89 south from Cameron. Again, watch for signs indicating the loop road through the two monuments.

ABOUT DAY-HIKING: Permits, even for day-hiking, are mandatory; *HIKING INTO THE BACKCOUNTRY IS PROHIBITED* without a permit issued at the Visitor Center. The permit must be returned to the Visitor Center after your hike

MONUMENT INFORMATION: Visitor Center (602-527-7040); details of hiking restrictions and necessary permits are also available here

CAMPGROUNDS: None in monument — the nearest is 20 miles southwest of Wupatki Visitor Center (Bonito Campground, adjacent to Sunset Crater National Monument)

REPORT EMERGENCIES: Visitor Center (527-7040) or any ranger

MONUMENT ADDRESS: Wupatki National Monument, HC 33, Box 444A, Flagstaff, Arizona 86001

WEATHER: Summers warm, with daytime highs in 90s and 100s, nightime lows in 60s. Winter days are cool (60s) and nights chilly (30s or lower). July and August thundershowers bring most of the area's rain.

DEADMAN WASH HIKE

DISTANCE: 3.5 miles one-way

TRAILHEAD: Overlook Picnic Area, 4 miles northwest of Visitor Center (sign on highway marked "Viewpoint and Lunch Area")

ELEVATION: Start 5300 feet; end 4900 feet; highest 5300 feet

GRADES: very easy

RANGER STATION: Visitor Center

BEST SEASONS: Spring or fall

PLANT COMMUNITY: Cool-desert scrub

COMMON PLANTS: Juniper, four-wing saltbush, rabbit-brush, prince's plume, sand sage, mormon tea, cliffrose

COMMON ANIMALS: blacktail jackrabbit, pronghorn antelope, antelope squirrel, horned lark, canyon wren, raven, red-tailed hawk, collared lizard, spiny lizard, whip-tail lizard

NOTE: There's no water along the trail — carry a full canteen; summer heat may make hiking uncomfortable at mid-day; the route is not an established trail, but is well-defined

The **DEADMAN WASH HIKE** begins at the Overlook picnic area; find an old but distinct road at the far end of the picnic area and follow it through an open juniper forest, enjoying fine views of the San Francisco Peaks. The road goes down a gentle grade into a small wash — follow the road's left fork.

A short walk takes you to the valley of Deadman Wash; follow the old road as it wanders downstream. Note the walls of lava on your left and the deep wash on your right. At about two miles a faint trail comes in on your left; stay on the main roadway, which soon meets the main wash. This is a good place to watch circling hawks and vultures.

In another mile the monument's boundary fence parallels the road, and within a quarter-mile Wupatki Ruin and the visitor center come into view as you top a small rise. Climb across a locked gate, then follow the road until you see a ruin (Wupatki's "ball court"). Don't take any shortcuts to the ball court or the main ruins — the intervening arroyos are unstable. From the ball court you can follow paved paths to the visitor center.

You can retrace your route to the Overlook picnic area, hitch a ride or arrange a car-shuttle back to your vehicle.

Wupatki National Monument   (NPS photo)

13

PETRIFIED FOREST NATIONAL PARK

Petrified Forest National Park occupies what was once a vast floodplain crossed by many meandering streams. At the headwaters of these streams grew forests of pine-like trees. Some of these trees were washed into the floodplain and were covered by silt, mud, and volcanic ash. Over time, ground water deposited minerals which penetrated the log's fibers — the petrified wood found in the area today is the result of that process. The fossil record available at Petrified Forest is exciting, since it includes not only plant material, but many animal remains as well; it's one of the few places where it may become possible to reconstruct a nearly complete fossil ecosystem. The erosional forces of wind and water have left plant and animal fossils exposed, giving the Senior hiker an unusual opportunity to look back across the millenia. One place where the hiker can see the process of erosion exposing fossil material is on the Blue Mesa Interpretive Trail — a short and interesting walk through the "badlands" of Petrified Forest.

GETTING THERE: If coming from the west on I-40, take US 180 at Holbrook to the park's south entrance — you can drive the park and rejoin I-40 at the north entrance. If coming from the east, leave I-40 at the north entrance, join US 180 at the south entrance and rejoin I-40 at Holbrook

ABOUT DAY-HIKING: No permit is necessary, but you must *LEAVE THE PARK BEFORE CLOSING TIME;* otherwise, get an overnight permit at either visitor center or at the park's entrance stations. Be aware of the park's closing time (the park remains on Mountain Standard Time throughout the year)

PARK PERMITS AND INFORMATION: Painted Desert Visitor Center (602-524-6228) and Rainbow Forest Museum (524-3015); both entrance stations

CAMPGROUNDS: None located in the park

REPORT EMERGENCIES: Either visitor center, any ranger, or by calling 524-6025

NEAREST PHYSICIAN: Holbrook or Winslow, Arizona; Gallup, New Mexico

PARK ADDRESS: Petrified Forest National Park, Petrified Forest National Park, Arizona 86028

WEATHER: Spring and fall are the best hiking seasons, with clear skies and moderate temperatures. Late summer brings thunderstorms, and winter brings cold temperatures and some snow. Temperatures vary from winter lows of around zero to summer highs near 100.

BLUE MESA INTERPRETIVE TRAIL

DISTANCE: 1.0 mile round-trip

TRAILHEAD: Blue Mesa spur road

ELEVATION: Start 5100 feet; highest 5100 feet

GRADES: Very easy (steep section at beginning and end)

RANGER STATION: Rainbow Forest Museum

BEST SEASONS: Spring or fall

PLANT COMMUNITY: Desert grassland, high plateau

COMMON PLANTS: Mormon tea, yucca, four-winged saltbush

COMMON ANIMALS: Coyote, antelope squirrel, collared lizard

NOTE: There's no water along the trail — carry an ample supply; summer heat may make mid-day hiking uncomfortable; there may be ice on trail in winter

The **BLUE MESA INTERPRETIVE TRAIL** winds through multicolored badlands; erosion has exposed layers of pale blue, white and reddish sediments on cone-shaped hills, ravines, ridges and small canyons. Because of the varying hardness of the layers, the cutting action of water has been uneven and irregular — the result is a landscape that's constantly changing yet remarkably stable in its main features. Petrified logs, undercut by erosion, rest atop small pillars of softer material until the pillars dissolve and the log tumbles.

Further erosion exposes other logs and the process repeats itself. Since erosion is occuring so rapidly, plants have little chance of becoming established and the badland area is nearly devoid of vegetaion. As if to make up for this lack, the slopes are patterned with a remarkable series of tiny ravines and gullies, well worth a closer look. The trail itself has an asphalt surface to keep it from eroding away. The path wanders through a small segment of the badlands formation and then returns to the parking area. Try this trail for a close-up view of some of the forces that have shaped this unusual landscape.

Navajo National Monument   (NPS photo)

14

NAVAJO
NATIONAL MONUMENT

For more than thirteen centuries the vast Colorado Plateau of Arizona, New Mexico, Colorado, and Utah was the home of the ancestors of today's modern Pueblo Indians. The Anasazi (Navajo for "the ancient ones") developed a civilization which is only beginning to be understood. One of the best ways to interpret this civilization for yourself is through a visit to Betatakin, in Navajo National Monument. The earliest inhabitants of the Kayenta area apparently wandered widely, making their living by hunting, gathering seeds and nuts, and growing some squash and corn. The details of their lives remain lost to us since they left little physical evidence to record their history.

By about 400 AD these early hunter-gatherers had perfected agriculture to such a point that they could profit by settling in one place. They began to build permanent structures, improved their farming techniques, increased in numbers, and apparently flourished.

In time three distinct cultural centers became dominant in the Four Corners area — Mesa Verde, Chaco Canyon and the area around Kayenta. As Anasazi civilization evolved in the 11th and 12th centuries larger towns and cities began to develop. Life must have been sweet on the Colorado Plateau in those days, with wealth and leisure enough for crafts and arts to become more and more important. First one cultural center dominated, then another. In the 11th century it was Chaco Canyon, in the 12th it was Mesa Verde. Kayenta's turn came in the 13th century, when the region around Navajo National Monument must have been the Athens of the Colorado Plateau.

But then, sometime before the 1300s, things changed for the Anasazi. Perhaps a cycle of drought accompanied by overpopulation and soil depletion, perhaps the pressure of raids by nomadic enemies and an increase in social pressures occurred, or perhaps a combination of all these factors caused the abandonment of the Anasazi cities. Whatever the reason, the people of Mesa Verde and Chaco Canyon evenutally migrated to the Rio Grande valley, and the Kayenta people moved southward into Hopi lands, leaving their cities to fall into ruins.

The remains of Betatakin give a glimpse into the lives of the Kayenta Anasazi. The building itself is tucked into a large sandstone alcove, where springs seep from the base of the cave. Betatakin was constructed during the 13th century, occupied for less than 50 years, then abandoned in the great exodus that occurred about 1300. Because of the fragility of the ruins, hikers can visit Betatakin only with a ranger, and the number of visitors in the area is carefully controlled.

GETTING THERE: The monument is nine miles off US 160, southwest of Kayenta, Arizona on AZ 564

ABOUT DAY-HIKING: A permit is required for all trails except the self-guided nature trail (check at Visitor Center for times of ranger-lead hikes to Betatakin)

MONUMENT INFORMATION AND PERMITS: Visitor Center (details about hiking restrictions also available here, or by calling 602-672-2366 or 672-2367)

CAMPGROUND: Main campground near Visitor Center (no open fires)

REPORT EMERGENCIES: Visitor Center (672-2366 or 672-2367) or any ranger

NEAREST PHYSICIAN: Kayenta or Tuba City, Arizona

MONUMENT ADDRESS: Navajo National Monument, HC 71, Box 3, Tonalea, AZ 86044

WEATHER: Summer highs in 90s, pleasantly cool at night. Afternoon thundershowers usual in July and August. Winter and spring are usually quite cold, with snow common.

BETATAKIN RUINS TRAIL

DISTANCE: 2.7 miles round-trip

TRAILHEAD: Ranger-conducted; get permit and meet at Visitor Center

ELEVATION: Start 7286 feet; end 7286 feet; lowest 6600 feet

GRADES: 700-foot steep section, remainder moderate

RANGER STATION: Visitor Center

BEST SEASONS: Late spring, summer, early fall

PLANT COMMUNITIES: Pinon pine-juniper forest on mesa top, riparian or streamside forest with aspen at ruins site

COMMON PLANTS: Cliffrose, buffaloberry, sage, narrowleaf mountain mahogany, mormon tea, meadow rue, narrowleaf and broadleaf yucca, prickly pear, gilia, penstemon

COMMON ANIMALS: Canyon wren, broad-tailed hummingbird, cottontail rabbit, rock squirrel, bobcat, coyote

NOTE: No water along the trail — carry ample supply; summer heat, winter cold; possibility of rockfall in areas off trail; loose gravel on some sections of trail

Tours for **BETATAKIN** leave from the visitor center several times a day during the summer season (sign up for tours early, since the number of hikers is strictly limited). After riding to the trailhead, hikers descend quickly through a series of switchbacks; the trail then turns up a small side-canyon, entering a delightful riparian forest more typical of higher, much cooler areas.

After walking through a fine grove of aspens and savoring the cool air of the canyon bottom, a short hike takes you to Betatakin. The ruins are located in an alcove where the overlying Navajo sandstone cliff meets the less porous Kayenta sandstone. Since the Kayenta sandstone greatly slows the movement of water, a series of springs and seeps has developed; this gave the people of Betatakin a fairly stable water supply. The ruins themselves are intriguing — they look as if the builders had simply walked away, as indeed they may have. The ranger accompanying your group will describe the main aspects of the ruin and discuss what is known of the Anasazi.

15

CANYON DE CHELLY NATIONAL MONUMENT

Canyon de Chelly National Monument encompasses a series of beautiful steep-walled canyons which sheltered prehistoric Pueblo Indians for some ten centuries, and later served as a stronghold for modern Navajo Indians. Anasazi ruins are perched on nearly inaccessible ledges or snuggled in alcoves in towering cliffs beside Canyon de Chelly and Canyon del Muerto, contrasting with the present-day Navajo Indian homes and fields scattered along the canyon floors. Since the monument is home to the Navajo, hiking is restricted, with only the trail to White House Ruin open to the general public. You must be accompanied by either a ranger or a Navajo guide for hikes into other areas of the monument. You'll enjoy the easy hike to White House Ruins — an especially well-preserved example of the architectural brilliance of a long-vanished people.

GETTING THERE: Canyon de Chelly is quite near Chinle, Arizona, which is on US 191 (the area's main north-south highway)

ABOUT DAY-HIKING: No permit required for hikes to White House Ruin (all other hikes must be accompanied by a ranger or authorized guide)

MONUMENT INFORMATION, PERMITS AND GUIDES: Visitor Center or by calling 602-674-5436

CAMPGROUND: Cottonwood Campground (located near Visitor Center; no fee)

REPORT EMERGENCIES: Visitor Center (674-5436 or 674-5213); Navajo Police (674-5291); ambulance service (674-5464)

NEAREST PHYSICIAN: Chinle (two miles from visitor center)

MONUMENT ADDRESS: Canyon de Chelly National Monument, Box 588, Chinle, Arizona 86503

WEATHER: May-September temperatures range from 40s at night to high in 90s during the day. Humidity low but afternoon thunderstorms common from July through August

WHITE HOUSE RUIN TRAIL

DISTANCE: 2.5 miles round-trip

TRAILHEAD: White House Overlook (on South Rim Drive)

ELEVATION: Start 6500 feet; end 6500 feet; lowest 5300 feet

GRADES: Moderate

RANGER STATION: Visitor Center

BEST SEASONS: Spring, summer, fall

PLANT COMMUNITIES: Cool desert grassland; riparian or streamside woodland

COMMON PLANTS: Juniper, pinon pine, prickly pear, Russian olive, cottonwood, tamarisk

COMMON ANIMALS: Canyon wren, cliff swallow, raven, racoon, cottontail, spiny lizard

NOTE: Surface water may be contaminated — carry ample supply of good water; smooth rock off trail may be slippery after a rain; hikers are asked not to enter or photograph hogans without permission

The **WHITE HOUSE RUIN TRAIL** starts at White House Overlook, then drops quickly through a series of switchbacks past sandstone cliffs with well-developed crossbedding. After a steady descent, the trail passes through a tunnel and emerges at a Navajo farm (the hogan is occupied — please don't approach or photograph it without permission).

The trail then goes to the river, with White House Ruins at the base of the sheer sandstone cliff across and slightly downstream from you. Wade the shallow creek, enjoying the sandy bottom and the coolness of the water after your hike. The banks of the stream support a fine riparian vegetation of cottonwoods, willows, and tamarisk. When you get to White House Ruins, take a few moments to imagine how the area must have looked eight centruies ago. There would have been fields of corn, beans and squash, and majestic cottonwoods lining the creek — but there would have been no tamarisk or Russian olive trees. Tamarisk and Russian olive were introduced to North America in the late ninteenth century — long after the disappearance of the Anasazi who built their cities in this mystical spot.

As you hike back to the rim, look again at the graceful sandstone cliff sweeping lightly above White House Ruin; think of how it must have influenced the people who lived there (and how they must have missed it when they left).

Canyon de Chelly National Monument (NPS photo)

16

CHACO CULTURE NATIONAL HISTORICAL PARK

Chaco Canyon is in the true high-desert, with long, cold winters, short, hot summers, and scanty rainfall. Yet a thousand years ago, when the climate was much the same as it is today, Chaco Canyon was a center of Anasazi culture and life. At the hub of a far-flung road network, ancient Chaco was the high-point of Anasazi social organization and community life, as well as architecture and probably religion.

By the 11th century Chaco Canyon may have had several thousand persons living in some 400 settlements in and around the main canyon — some of the larger structures had walls rising five stories, hundreds of rooms, and scores of kivas or ceremonial chambers. Perhaps Chaco Canyon was the Anasazi "capital" of the region, serving as an economic and political center for the surrounding towns, storing food and trade goods and dominating the social and religious affairs of the area. Why, then, was Chaco Canyon abandoned?

Its decline coincides with a prolonged drought in the 12th century; perhaps lack of rainfall combined with overpopulation resulted in food shortages followed by disruption of the social fabric of the region. Whatever the reasons, the people of Chaco Canyon left behind impressive evidence of their once-great culture. The best way to recapture the glory of Anasazi life and architecture is to hike among the ruins of the canyon. A good place to start is with the Penasco Blanco Trail.

GETTING THERE: From the north, turn off NM 44 at Nageezi Trading Post, then follow NM 57 to the north entrance. If coming from the south and I-40 take NM 57 at Thoreau for 44 miles; at a marked junction turn onto a dirt road — follow it 20 miles to the south entrance (call the visitor center at 505-786-5384 or inquire locally about the condition of the dirt road before attempting it)

ABOUT DAY-HIKING: No permit is required for hikes in the canyon proper — *A PERMIT IS REQUIRED FOR HIKES ON THE SURROUNDING MESAS.* All major ruins have self-guiding trails beginning at adjacent parking areas. Permits are available at the Visitor Center (505-786-5384) or from any field ranger

PARK INFORMATION: Visitor Center (505-786-5384)

CAMPGROUND: Gallo Campground, one mile east of Visitor Center (no fee; no motorhomes or trailers longer than 32 feet)

REPORT EMERGENCIES: Visitor Center (786-5384) or any ranger

NEAREST PHYSICIAN: Bloomfield and Aztec, New Mexico

PARK ADDRESS: Chaco Culture National Historical Park, Star Route 4, Box 6500, Bloomfield, New Mexico 87413

WEATHER: Summer days hot, evenings cool (frost has been recorded in every month but July). Summer afternoon thunderstorms are common; winters cold and dry. Humidity low year-round; annual precipitation averages about 8.5 inches.

PENASCO BLANCO TRAIL

DISTANCE: 4.4 miles round-trip

TRAILHEAD: Casa Chiquita (4.2 miles northwest of Visitor Center)

ELEVATION: Start 6111 feet; highest 6300 feet

GRADES: Easy, with one very short moderate section

RANGER STATION: Visitor Center

BEST SEASONS: Late spring, early and late summer, early fall

PLANT COMMUNITIES: Sage, riparian or streamside

COMMON PLANTS: Pigweed, bee-weed, saltbush, shadscale, greasewood, rabbitbush, mormon tea, globe mallow, cottonwood, sagebrush, snakeweed

COMMON ANIMALS: Collared lizard, side-blotched lizard, turkey vulture, raven, rock wren, canyon wren, brown towhee, ground squirrel, coyote, cottontail, jackrabbit, prairie dog

NOTE: There are no water sources along the trail — carry an ample supply of water; be prepared for intense heat and solar radiation during warmer periods

The **PENASCO BLANCO TRAIL** follows an old wagon road down Chaco Canyon from the ruins of Casa Chiquita. As you hike the first portion of the trail, examine the rocks along the right side of the canyon for petroglyphs (please don't touch) of bighorn sheep, human figures, geometric designs and other elements.

As the trail crosses Chaco Wash and begins to climb to the south mesa, look for a faint trail on your right. This trail leads to an overhang with red pictographs of a crescent moon, a star and a human hand. The star and moon may represent a supernova visible at Chaco in 1054 AD. After viewing the pictograph, return to the main trail, climb to the mesa-top and walk the short distance to the ruins of Penasco Blanco.

This pueblo has an unusual elliptical layout, and had over 150 rooms on the ground floor alone. Parts of the structure were three stories high. Unusual, too, are the numbers of great kivas associated with Penasco Blanco; you can see the remains of two great kivas within the enclosed plaza, and two more to the south and the northwest. Construction probably started in the early 900s and lasted for at least 200 years. Look for evidence of changing masonry styles, from simple slab walls to chinked and banded compound walls to rubble-core walls with a fine veneer.

Take your time to look around, imagining how life must have been in ancient Penasco Blanco, then return to the trailhead by retracing your route to Casa Chiquita (remember to stay on the trail — don't take short-cuts).

17

BANDELIER
NATIONAL MONUMENT

Bandelier National Monument is best known for its remarkable cliff dwellings and pre-Columbian ruins, and it's no wonder — there are numerous archaeological sites within the monument. The largest and most impressive are in the beautiful little canyon of the Rito de los Frijoles, and can be seen on an easy walk from the Visitor Center. Bandelier National Monument is located on the Pajarito Plateau, an area of tuff (consolidated volcanic ash blown out of one of the world's largest calderas) and basaltic lava from a different eruption. In fact, the Jemez Mountains constitute the rim of an ancient volcano.

Apparently Frijoles Canyon was inhabited from about the late 12th century through the late Sixteenth Century. The inhabitants of the canyon built some of their dwellings by enlarging holes in the easily-worked tuff of the cliff walls, and built a large pueblo in the valley bottom. They grew beans, corn and squash in the fertile valley and on the mesas, but abandoned the area sometime in the 1500's; tradition links the Anasazi people of the area with several of the existing Rio Grande pueblos.

You can take an hour's walk through Frijoles Canyon on a loop trail starting at the visitor center for a sample of Bandelier's ruins. It's a walk well worth taking. While best known for its archaeological sites, Bandelier is mostly undisturbed wilderness. Two of my favorite hikes here are the walk from Ponderosa Campground via Upper Frijoles Crossing to the Visitor Center, and from the Visitor Center to the Rio Grande River and back.

GETTING THERE: From Santa Fe go north on US 285, then turn west on NM 4 to the monument's entrance

ABOUT DAY-HIKING: A free permit is required for all trails except Falls and Frey Trails and trails near the Visitor Center; permits are issued at the visitor center or by phone (call 505-672-3861)

MONUMENT INFORMATION: Visitor Center (672-3861)

CAMPGROUNDS: Juniper Campground (located near Entrance Station); Ponderosa Campground (groups only, reservation required; located four miles west of the entrance station)

REPORT EMERGENCIES: Visitor Center (672-3861 from 8 am to 5 pm; 672-3862 or 672-3863 after 5 pm)

NEAREST PHYSICIAN: Los Alamos, New Mexico

MONUMENT ADDRESS: Bandelier National Monument, Los Alamos, New Mexico 87544

WEATHER: May-September temperatures from 50s at night to high in 80s during the day. Low relative humidity; thunderstorms usual in afternoon during July and August.

FALLS-RIO GRANDE TRAIL

DISTANCE: 1.5 miles one-way to Falls, 2.4 miles one-way to Rio Grande

TRAILHEAD: Backpacker's parking area near visitor center

ELEVATION: Start 6066 feet; end 5391 feet; highest 6066 feet

GRADES: Moderate with several steeper sections

RANGER STATION: Visitor Center (self-guiding geology trail book is available there)

BEST SEASONS: Year-round

PLANT COMMUNITY: Riparian or streamside

COMMON PLANTS: Narrowleaf cottonwoods, ponderosa pine, Gambel oak, chokecherry, desert olive, mormon tea, sage

COMMON ANIMALS: Abert squirrel, Audubon's cottontail, rock squirrel, Colorado chipmunk, raccoon, coyote, Turkey vulture, red-tailed hawk

NOTE: Surface water may be contaminated — carry good water; there may be poison ivy in areas off the trail

The **FALLS TRAIL** begins among stately ponderosa pines at the east end of the Visitor Center parking area, near the section reserved for backpacker's vehicles. It then crosses an open slope and parallels the stream. Within the first mile it passes lava flows and tentrocks — the remnants of fumaroles or passages left by escaping gases when hot ash was laid down by eruptions of the Jemez volcano.

The trail climbs a south slope to pass the narrow canyon where the creek cascades over Upper Falls. The trail is lined with ponderosa pines, Gamble oaks, cottonwoods, boxelders, and chokecherrys, with mormon tea, sage and rabbitbush in the drier areas. The trail continues to descend, passing Lower Falls and finally reaching the Rio Grande river — now part of the man-made Cochiti Lake. The dead trees are a result of fluctuations in the water level as the lake alternately floods and recedes, leaving new soil which supports many weedy species but kills the native vegetation along the shore. The fence just upriver from the mouth of the Rito de los Frijoles is the boundary between the monument and adjacent Department of Energy land.

Return to the visitor center parking area by retracing your route to the river, and enjoy some different views of the Lower and Upper Falls.

FRIJOLES CANYON TRAIL

DISTANCE: 7.3 miles one-way

TRAILHEAD: Ponderosa Group Campground, four miles west of park's entrance station

ELEVATION: Start 7610 feet; end 6066 feet; highest 7610 feet

GRADES: Easy with one steep downhill section

RANGER STATION: Visitor Center

BEST SEASONS: Spring, summer, fall

PLANT COMMUNITIES: Ponderosa pine, riparian or streamside

COMMON PLANTS: Ponderosa pine, meadow rue, horsetail rush, valerian, cottonwood, boxelder, choke-cherry, sage, gambel oak

COMMON ANIMALS: Least chipmunk, Colorado chipmunk, Abert squirrel, rock squirrel, deer mouse, coyote, broadtailed hummingbird, flicker, hairy woodpecker, scrub jay, Stellar jay, white-breasted nuthatch

NOTE: Surface water may be contaminated — carry good water; poison ivy and stinging nettles may be found in areas off the trail

It's best to start hiking the **FRIJOLES CANYON TRAIL** knowing you have a second vehicle waiting for you at the visitor center, since returning to Ponderosa Campground involves a steep 400-foot climb out of Frijoles Canyon. The trail starts in a burned-over ponderosa pine forest, the result of the La Mesa fire of 1977. The burned area is rapidly being reclaimed by flowering plants. The trail's first mile is on a level fire road, followed by a 400-foot descent into Frijoles Canyon. The trail then follows the course of the stream all the way to the visitor center. Be prepared to get your feet wet, since there are some thirty stream crossings between this point and the visitor center.

As you hike enjoy the lush riparian vegetation, including horsetail rushes, ferns, boxelders and other plants typical of cool, moist habitats. Use care if you hike off the trail, though, since poison ivy and stinging nettles grow in the same environment you're enjoying.

About a mile and a half above the visitor center, the canyon suddenly widens around you, and another few minutes hiking takes you to the Ceremonial Cave area; Ceremonial Cave itself is an overhang 150 feet above the canyon floor; the overhang is accessible by a series of wooden ladders. Take a few minutes to climb up and look over the kiva or ceremonial chamber there. You'll also notice a series of viga sockets which show the former location of several small rooms. The Visitor Center is a pleasant one-mile hike from Ceremonial Cave.

Take the last mile slowly, enjoying the lovely valley and viewing the cliff-dwellings left by the ancient Anasazi. Watch, too, for black or gray Abert's squirrels and mule deer — they're very much at home in the monument (remember not to feed or disturb them). You'll like this hike — it's one of the most pleasant in the Southwest.

18

WHITE SANDS NATIONAL MONUMENT

White Sands National Monument, in the downfaulted Tularosa Basin, is overlooked by rugged mountains to the east and west. Eroding through the centuries, gypsum from these mountains is carried to Lake Lucero in the lowest part of the basin. When the gypsum-laden water evaporates the white mineral can be carried by dry southwest winds to areas where the wind slows enough to drop its load of airborne particles. There, bit by bit, sand-sized gypsum grains accumulate to form dunes. Pushed by the wind, each dune grows and moves further and further from the gypsum flats and the drying lake; new dunes form and the process is repeated, resulting in the slow march of dunes across the floor of the basin. White Sands National Monument contains some of the most impressive of these dune areas, along with those plants and animals able to survive in a harsh and constantly changing environment. Hiking the dunes is a unique experience — one you won't forget.

GETTING THERE: The monument is on US 70-82, southwest of Alamogordo or northeast of Las Cruces, New Mexico

ABOUT DAY-HIKING: No permits are needed, but you may inform rangers of your hiking plans

MONUMENT INFORMATION: Visitor Center (505-437-1058)

CAMPGROUNDS: None in the monument (inquire about nearby USFS, New Mexico State Park and BLM campgrounds)

REPORT EMERGENCIES: Visitor Center (437-1058) or to any ranger

NEAREST PHYSICIAN: Alamogordo, New Mexico

MONUMENT ADDRESS: White Sands National Monument, Box 458, Alamogordo, New Mexico 88310

WEATHER: The area is subject to harsh and changing weather conditions. Summer days average 95 to 100, winters are mild but nightly lows are often below freezing. High winds may occur between February and May.

BIG DUNE TRAIL

DISTANCE: 1.0 mile round-trip

TRAILHEAD: Parking area three miles from the visitor center along the Heart of the Sands Loop Drive

ELEVATION: Start 4000 feet; highest 4050 feet

GRADES: Nearly level; two short steep climbs up the dunes

RANGER STATION: Visitor Center

BEST SEASONS: Fall or late spring

PLANT COMMUNITIES: Dune communities

COMMON PLANTS: Four-wing saltbush, soaptree yucca, rabbitbrush, Rio Grande cottonwood

COMMON ANIMALS: Bleached earless lizard, whiptail lizard, darkling beetles

NOTE: No water is available beyond the visitor center — carry a full canteen; summer heat; possibility of high winds in spring

The **BIG DUNE TRAIL** gives a good overview of White Sands National Monument. Plants to watch for include four-wing saltbush (an indicator of alkaline soil) and soaptree yucca (New Mexico's state flower). This yucca is pollinated by the pronuba moth which lays its eggs in the yucca's flower. The moth larvae eat some of the developing seeds, a small price to pay for assured pollination. Watch also for rice grass, a staple food of the original Indian inhabitants of the White Sands region.

As the trail wanders over the dunes, look for stands of Rio Grande cottonwoods — an unlikely inhabitant of such an arid-looking place. More common desert plants are mormon tea, skunkbush sumac and rabbitbrush. The views along the trail are impressive, with white, snowlike dunes in the foreground and distant, rugged mountains on the horizon. Near the end of the loop the trail goes through an area littered with fossilized plant roots; the roots were once encased in gypsum sand pedestals. "Living" pedestals can be seen a bit further down the trail. The roots in these pedestals may also undergo fossilization, to the delight of future monument visitors.

The trail descends the face of a large dune to bring you back to your vehicle.

BACKCOUNTRY CAMPSITE TRAIL

DISTANCE: 2.0 miles round-trip

TRAILHEAD: Signed parking area on the Heart of Sands Loop Drive five miles from the visitor center

ELEVATION: Start 4000 feet; highest 4040 feet

GRADES: Rolling but nearly level

RANGER STATION: Visitor Center

BEST SEASON: Fall

PLANT COMMUNITIES: Dune communities

COMMON PLANTS: Rio Grande cottonwood, soaptree yucca, mormon tea

COMMON ANIMALS: Mourning doves, bleached earless lizard, whiptail lizard, western kingbird, loggerhead shrike, darkling beetle

NOTE: No water is available beyond the visitor center — take a full canteen; summer heat may be a problem at mid-day

The trail to the only **BACKCOUNTRY CAMPSITE** in the monument begins at a well-marked parking area, then climbs the face of a large dune. The trail is marked by a series of ten numbered posts, each placed within sight of the next, making route-finding an easy task.

The trail meanders up and down a series of dunes, then through a group of gypsum pedestals. The trail passes several interdunal flats, each with a proliferation of bunchgrasses growing in the relatively moist low areas. The trail continues across waves of dunes until it reachs the backcountry campsite, a pleasant spot near a grove of isolated Rio Grande cottonwoods.

Follow the trail back to the parking area and your vehicle. As you hike back, watch for whiptail and spiny lizards — they tend to be lighter in color here than elsewhere, a good example of protective coloration. This trail can be hot during the summer, or even on fall and spring afternoons. Take plenty of water as well as film — White Sands is not only hot and dry, it's also a photographer's paradise.

White Sands National Monument   (NPS photo)

Guadalupe Mountain National Park   (NPS photo)

19

GUADALUPE MOUNTAINS NATIONAL PARK

Guadalupe Mountains National Park is one of those wonderful surprises Senior hikers sometimes come across as they travel the Southwest. The park is an outpost of cool, green canyons and forested mountains swimming in a sea of desert. Miles of well-marked and well-maintained trails lead from warm desert up into cooler, greener forests with isolated springs, past intriguing geologic formations, historic sites and quiet areas with unsurpassed views of distant deserts and canyons. North and south meet here, a place where pines and firs from the Rockies exist side-by side with madrone and cacti from the southern deserts. The feeling is that of being on the frontier, at a place where two great landscapes come together. Guadalupe is a day-hiker's park — you'll enjoy its quiet beauty as you begin to learn its story. A good way to start is with two of my favorite hikes; one to "the most beautiful place in Texas", the other to a cool spring hidden in a lovely canyon.

GETTING THERE: Frijole Visitor Center is the best place to start a visit to Guadalupe Mountains National Park; it's located on US 62-180, 55 miles southwest of Carlsbad, NM, or 110 miles east of El Paso, TX. If coming from Big Bend, Guadalupe can be approached on TX 54 via Van Horn, TX.

ABOUT DAY-HIKING: Sign the trail register at the trailhead; discuss any unusual plans with rangers at Frijole Visitor Center (915-828-3251)

PARK INFORMATION: Frijole Visitor Center (915-828-3251)

CAMPGROUNDS: Pine Spring, 1.8 miles west of Frijole Visitor Center; Dog Canyon (125 miles by road from Frijole Visitor Center)

REPORT EMERGENCIES: Frijole Visitor Center (828-3251); check park bulletin bulletin boards for other numbers to call), McKittrick Canyon Visitor Center, campground host or any ranger

NEAREST PHYSICIAN: Carlsbad, New Mexico

PARK ADDRESS: Guadalupe Mountains National Park, Star Route 1, Box 480, Carlsbad, NM 88220

WEATHER: Climate is semi-arid, with most precipitation falling in the summer and early fall (although there may be snowstorms during the winter months). Summer highs are usually in the upper 80s, winter highs in the 50s. High winds can occur at any time, but are most frequent in the spring and fall. Be prepared for sudden changes in weather conditions.

McKITTRICK CANYON TRAIL TO PRATT CABIN

DISTANCE: 4.6 miles round-trip

TRAILHEAD: McKittrick Canyon Visitor Center

ELEVATION: Start 5000 feet; highest 5200 feet

GRADES: Very easy

RANGER STATION: McKittrick Canyon Visitor Center (if closed, Frijole Visitor Center)

BEST SEASONS: Spring, summer, fall

PLANT COMMUNITIES: Riparian or streamside; high desert

COMMON PLANTS: Big-tooth maple, sawgrass, sotol, cholla, alligator and red-berry juniper, prickly pear, ponderosa pine, little walnut, common chokecherry

COMMON ANIMALS: Whiptail and spiny lizards, scrub jay, canyon and cactus wren, grayheaded junco, Townsend's solitaire, rock squirrel, porcupine, ringtail cat, hognosed skunk

NOTE: The gate at the highway is locked at a designated time (you must be at the highway before the gate is closed in the evening)

The **McKITTRICK CANYON TRAIL** to the Pratt cabin begins just behind the McKittrick Canyon Visitor Center. It follows the stream's course for the entire distance, crossing the streambed several times before coming to the cabin and picnic area. The first part of the trail takes you through vegetation typical of the Chihuahuan desert — yucca, agave, juniper, scrub oak, sotol and cacti. Beyond the first crossing the vegetation changes, responding to cooler, moister conditions. Watch for big-tooth maples, ponderosa pines, chinkapin oaks and other plants typical of mountain streams in the southern Rockies.

Notice, too, that the stream bed, while dry in some places, is water-filled in others. Travertine, a mineral deposited by calcium carbonate-laden water, cements the streambed, forcing water to flow over the surface but allowing it to disappear underground wherever the travertine is broken. The travertime was damaged by boulders rolling along the streambed during floods; this now allows water to seep into lower levels of the bed — still there, but out of sight. Remember, the travertine layer can also be damaged by hikers, so please stay on the trail — don't risk altering the canyon's environment by wading or swimming in the water.

The trail approaching Pratt Cabin is shaded and cool — truly one of the most beautiful places in Texas. At the picnic area take a short trail to the right to visit Pratt Cabin, an interesting building in a lovely setting. If you want to see more of the canyon, continue another mile upstream, then take the left fork to the J.C. Hunter picnic area. Remember, though, that you must allow time to return to the trailhead and the highway before the road closes in the evening.

SMITH SPRING-MANZANITA SPRING TRAIL

DISTANCE: 2.3 miles round-trip

TRAILHEAD: Frijole Historic Site (0.5 miles north of Frijole Visitor Center)

ELEVATION: Start 5550 feet; highest 6100 feet

GRADES: Easy with one short moderate section

RANGER STATION: Frijole Visitor Center

BEST SEASONS: Spring, summer, fall

PLANT COMMUNITIES: High desert; riparian or streamside

COMMON PLANTS: Texas madrone, pinon pine, ponderosa pine, big-tooth maple, soaptree yucca, sotol, agave, prickly pear, scrub oak

COMMON ANIMALS: Mule deer, elk, coyote, scrub jay, mourning dove, western kingbird, whiptail and side-blotched lizards

NOTE: There's no safe water on the trail — be sure to carry a full canteen of good water

The **SMITH SPRING-MANZANITA SPRING TRAIL** starts in typically Chihuahuan Desert vegetation, with cholla, prickly pear, junipers, agave, sotol and scrub oak. The trail crosses several small washes (look for Texas madrone and pinon pines in the washes), passes the junction with the Bear Canyon Trail (stay on the right-hand trail), then goes gently up and around the shoulder of a ridge before entering a larger shady wash. There are fine views of El Capitan, Guadalupe Peak and Nipple Hill from the side of the open ridge. The trail descends into the wash and soon comes to Smith Spring, a cool spot in the desert heat, with ponderosa pines, Texas madrone, big-tooth maples, chinkapin oaks and maidenhair ferns in the well-watered canyon. Spend a few moments here — it's a magic place.

To go on to Manzanita Spring, follow the trail from the base of the mountains back out onto the desert. For a portion of the distance to Manzanita Spring, the path goes along the edge of a wash, giving a tree-top view of the vegetation inside the arroyo. There are also fine views of Nipple Hill and of the distant Permian Basin. You'll soon come to Manzanita Spring, the site of a heated battle between the US Calvary and the Mescalero Apaches. Manzanita Spring is a good place to spot wildlife; it's very different from Smith Spring — the habitat at Manzanita Spring is open and much warmer.

After spending a few moments at the spring, hike to your vehicle at Frijole Historic Site, and spend a little time in the delicious shade of the large trees surrounding the ranch's well-preserved buildings.

20

BIG BEND
NATIONAL PARK

The best way to enjoy Big Bend National Park is by hiking several of its many trails. Big Bend is wild country, so pay special attention to proper preparation — including always carrying plenty of water. You can't count on desert springs or water holes, so be sure to carry at least one gallon per person per day, and always inform a reliable party of your plans and time of return. Big Bend is a wonderful place, a land of desert, mountain and river. You'll enjoy making its acquaintance. There are two trails I especially recommend for Senior hikers just discovering the park: Lost Mine Trail and the Santa Elena Canyon Trail. One introduces the Chisos Mountains, a land of distant views and intimate canyons; the other invites you to sample a "linear oasis" beside the Rio Grande and to marvel at the power of one of the west's most important rivers. You'll enjoy them both.

GETTING THERE: US 385 comes to the park's north entrance from Marathon, Texas; TX 118 from Alpine comes to the west entrance; another route to the west entrance is from Marfa to Presidio on US 67, then to Study Butte on Ranch Road 170, then TX 118 to the park

ABOUT DAY-HIKING: Permits are not needed, but check with ranger stations and visitor centers for up-to-date information on hiking and trail conditions

PARK INFORMATION: Panther Junction Visitor Center (915-477-2251); Rio Grande Village Visitor Center (winter only); Basin Visitor Contact Station; Castolon Ranger Station; Persimmon Gap Entrance Station

CAMPGROUNDS: Chisos Basin Campground, Cottonwood Campground, Rio Grande Village Campground

REPORT EMERGENCIES: Any visitor center, ranger station, any ranger or employee, or call 477-2251 during business hours; see park bulletin boards for night-time emergency phone numbers

NEAREST PHYSICIAN: Paramedic services at Study Butte, Texas

PARK ADDRESS: Big Bend National Park, Texas 79834

WEATHER: Plenty of sunshine year-round; winter highs are in 60s, lows in mid-30s. Summer highs are in 90s, lows in mid-60s. Higher elevations will be 5-10 degrees cooler, lower elevations average 5-10 degrees warmer. The "rainy season" is from mid-June through October, and may bring danger of flash flooding. Humidity, of course, is quite low throughout the year.

LOST MINE TRAIL

DISTANCE: 4.8 miles round-trip

TRAILHEAD: Lost Mine Trailhead on the Chisos Basin Road

ELEVATION: Start 5600 feet; highest 6850 feet

GRADES: Very moderate with one steeper section

RANGER STATION: Chisos Basin Ranger Station

BEST SEASONS: Year-round

PLANT COMMUNITY: Pinon-juniper woodland

COMMON PLANTS: Alligator and drooping juniper, cholla, oaks, pinon pine, lechuguilla, prickly pear, agave, royal sage

COMMON ANIMALS: White-tailed deer, javelina, grey fox, peregrine falcon, grey-breasted jay, canyon wren, brown towhee

NOTE: No water is available on this trail — carry an ample supply; hiking off-trail is difficult — stay on the trail

The **LOST MINE TRAIL** begins at the Lost Mine trailhead on the Chisos Basin Road, where oaks, pinon pines, junipers, agaves, prickly pears and grasses line the lower portions of the trail. Watch for prickly pear with bites taken from their pads — javelina or peccary like to make meals of the moist flesh of the plant.

The forest soon opens to views of Green Gulch and the distant Rosillos Mountains, with the mass of Lost Mine Peak guarding the entrance to the Chisos Mountains. There are also good views up-canyon as the trail winds along the slope above Panther Pass. Skunkbush sumac and drooping juniper line the trail here — the drooping juniper looks like it needs water, but is actually well-adapted to desert and semidesert conditions. Note the differences in vegetation between the cooler and slightly more moist north-facing slopes and the warmer, drier south-facing hillsides. The trail soon comes to a divide overlooking Juniper Canyon — peregrine falcons may nest on the sheer walls of Casa Grande, the massive peak overlooking the divide. Be sure to stay on the trail in this area; don't disturb the falcons.

The Lost Mine Trail continues to climb, passing fragrant ash, ocotillo, royal sage, agave, sotol and Texas madrone. After a series of easy switchbacks, the trail ends at a saddle — great views here of Lost Mine Peak to the northeast, Crown Mountain to the southeast, and distant mountains and plains through the "keyholes" of nearby valleys.

Follow the trail back down to your vehicle, stopping again to look for peregrine falcons flying over Juniper Canyon. You'll like this pleasant and shady trail, especially during the hotter parts of the year.

SANTA ELENA CANYON TRAIL

DISTANCE: 1.7 miles round-trip

TRAILHEAD: End of Santa Elena Road

ELEVATION: Start 2146 feet; highest 2175 feet

GRADES: Very easy

RANGER STATION: Castolon Ranger Station

BEST SEASONS: Fall, winter, spring

PLANT COMMUNITY: Riparian

COMMON PLANTS: Cottonwood, tamarisk, common reed, desert willow, mesquite, hechtia, lechuguilla

COMMON ANIMALS: Canyon wren, raven, cliff swallow, coyote, whiptail lizard

NOTE: Surface water may be contaminated — carry good water with you; you may have to go upstream to find a an easy crossing of Terlingua Creek when the water is high

The **SANTA ELENA CANYON TRAIL** begins in a thick grove of mesquite and tamarisk at the end of the Santa Elena Canyon Road. Birds are drawn to this area, and your chances of seeing some rare or infrequent species from south of the border are very good here (as they are elsewhere in the park).

The trail soon opens into the floodplain of the Rio Grande and Terlingua Creek, where you can get a close look at the narrowest part of the Rio Grande's channel — the mouth of Santa Elena Canyon. Cross Terlingua Creek, going upstream to find an easy crossing place (if the flow seems deep and swift, put off hiking the rest of the trail until your next visit). On the other side of Terlingua Creek the trail is a floodproof walkway which climbs the side of the bluff as a series of stairs before sloping gradually back down to the water's edge. The trail closely follows the riverside through dense thickets of riparian vegetation, including bamboo-like common rush and tamarisk trees. Listen for the calls of canyon wrens and watch for signs of beaver and muskrat which may live in or along the river.

The trail passes beneath large boulders fallen from the cliffs above, then comes to a point where the cliffs reach the water in a sheer face. This deep gorge is one of the narrowest places in the seven-mile length of Santa Elena Canyon.

Retrace your route to return to your vehicle, and think about stopping at the old town of Castolon for a cool drink.

Big Bend National Park   (NPS photo)

SENIOR HIKER'S CHECKLIST

Use this checklist to record the dates of your hikes in the Southwestern national parks and monuments:

Trail: _____
Park: _____ Date: _____
Plants and animals seen: _____
Weather: _____
Notes: _____
_____
_____

Trail: _____
Park: _____ Date: _____
Plants and animals seen: _____
Weather: _____
Notes: _____
_____
_____

Trail: _____
Park: _____ Date: _____
Plants and animals seen: _____
Weather: _____
Notes: _____
_____
_____

Trail: _____
Park: _____ Date: _____
Plants and animals seen: _____
Weather: _____
Notes: _____
_____
_____

Trail: _____
Park: _____ Date: _____
Plants and animals seen: _____
Weather: _____
Notes: _____
_____
_____

Trail: _____
Park: _____ Date: _____
Plants and animals seen: _____
Weather: _____
Notes: _____
_____
_____

Trail: _____
Park: _____ Date: _____
Plants and animals seen: _____
Weather: _____
Notes: _____
_____
_____

Cut along the line and mail.